THE CRITICS DEBATE

General Editor: Michael Scott

THE WINTER'S TALE

Bill Overton

HUMANITIES PRESS INTERNATIONAL, INC.
Atlantic Highlands, NJ

First published in 1989 in the United States of America by
HUMANITIES PRESS INTERNATIONAL INC., Atlantic
Highlands, NJ 07716

Library of Congress Cataloging-in-Publication Data

Overton, Bill
    The winter's tale

    (The Critics debate)
    Bibliography: p.
    Includes index.
    1. Shakespeare, William, 1564–1616. Winter's tale.
I. Title.   II. Series.
PR2839.094   1989 C.2 822.3′3   88–8242
ISBN 0–391–03613–0
ISBN 0–391–03614–9 (pbk.)

PRINTED IN HONG KONG

5

Contents

General Editor's Preface

OVER THE last few years the practice of literary criticism has become hotly debated. Methods developed earlier in the century and before have been attacked and the word "crisis" has been drawn upon to describe the present condition of English Studies. That such a debate is taking place is a sign of the subject discipline's health. Some would hold that the situation necessitates a radical alternative approach which naturally implies a "crisis situation". Others would respond that to employ such terms is to precipitate or construct a false position. The debate continues but it is not the first. "New Criticism" acquired its title because it attempted something fresh, calling into question certain practices of the past. Yet the practices it attacked were not entirely lost or negated by the new critics. One factor becomes clear: English Studies is a pluralistic discipline.

What are students coming to advanced work in English for the first time to make of all this debate and controversy? They are in danger of being overwhelmed by the cross-currents of critical approaches as they take up their study of literature. The purpose of this series is to help delineate various critical approaches to specific literary texts. Its authors are from a variety of critical schools and have approached their task in a flexible manner. Their aim is to help the reader come to terms with the variety of criticism and to introduce him or her to further reading on the subject and to a fuller evaluation of a particular text by illustrating the way it has been approached in a number of contexts. In the first part of the book a critical survey is given of some of the major ways the text has been appraised. This is done sometimes in a thematic manner, sometimes according to various "schools" or "approaches". In the second part the authors provide their own appraisals of the text from their stated critical standpoint, allowing the reader the knowledge of their own particular approaches from which their views may in turn be evaluated. The series therein hopes to introduce and to elucidate criticism of authors and texts being studied and to encourage participation as the critics debate.

Michael Scott

Acknowledgements

I WANT to thank the staff of Loughborough University Library for their help, especially the Inter-Library Loan Department; and also the Shakespeare Centre at Stratford-upon-Avon for allowing me access to books and archives.

Among individuals I am especially grateful to John Lucas for the stimulus of his essay on *The Winter's Tale* and for subsequent talk; to Michael Scott, General Editor of the series; and to Jim Friedman, David Fussell, Robin Hamilton and my wife Susan. All of these helped improve the book by reading and commenting on it in draft. Its remaining shortcomings are mine.

Bill Overton

A Note on Text and References

ALL quotations from *The Winter's Tale* are from the New Penguin Shakespeare edition by Ernest Schanzer (1969). Quotations from other plays by Shakespeare are from *The Complete Works* edited by Peter Alexander (1951).

References to works of criticism are identified by the name of the author and the date of publication. Page numbers are given in brackets after quotations. Where no numbers appear the reference is the one given immediately before or after. Several of the critical works discussed have been reprinted in full or part in Kenneth Muir's *Casebook* on *The Winter's Tale* (London, 1968). References are made to this whenever possible, and are indicated by the name *Casebook* and the page number(s).

Full bibliographical details are provided in the *References* section at the end. For convenience in referring to works discussed in Part One, this is divided according to each of its ten sections, with added to most of these a number of titles for further reading. All other works referred to are included in a general section at the end.

Introduction

LAURA Bohannan, an American anthropologist, once attempted to tell the story of *Hamlet* to a remote Nigerian tribe, the Tiv (1956). She began from two assumptions: that human nature the world over is much the same, and that classic works can cross boundaries of language and culture. If either of these assumptions can be said to have survived her experiment, it must be in a very different way from what she expected. The Tiv found the story of *Hamlet* full of interest. This, however, was not as Laura Bohannan told it but as they understood it, according to their own knowledge and beliefs. Not only did they soon intervene to correct her, according to the way they saw the world around them, but by the end they had taken over the story and its interpretation completely.

This anthropological anecdote is a suitable starting point because it illustrates the place of verbal art in a society and the place of interpretation and criticism. Verbal art is one of the main ways in which people make sense of themselves and their lives. But words always occur in contexts; despite appearances, they are never self-sufficient. For Laura Bohannan the context of *Hamlet* included not only an idea of Shakespeare and an idea of literature – lacking to the Tiv whose culture was wholly oral. Still more it included all the other cultural baggage which she had brought with her from America and Europe, and which, for the most part instinctively, had enabled her to form an understanding of the play.

I say 'an understanding' because no interpretation is ever complete or definitive. *Hamlet* is a part of Western culture as it was not of Tiv culture. Nevertheless a cultural gap still lies between it and a Western audience or reader today. Interpretation is a bridge across that gap, raised on each side upon different foundations of thought and belief. The foundations supplied by the Tiv were so different that for them it was quite right for Claudius, especially as king, to marry Gertrude as soon as possible after his brother's death. This puts an unusual complexion upon *Hamlet*, though one which in its own terms is apt, coherent and convincing. But in responding to the play, told as a story, the Tiv were not only making sense of it in their own way. Story-telling was for them less a way of passing time in the rainy season than a kind of moral teach-in. The elder men led the discussion, pointing occasional loaded remarks at their juniors and women. In doing so they reinforced the moral code and systems of belief of which they were the guardians. This activity, not always easy to distinguish from interpretation, is one important meaning of the word 'criticism'.

There are obvious and important differences between the practice of criticism in an industrialised, literate culture and in that of the Tiv. The critical debate is usually written rather than oral, and it is both more varied and less authoritarian. But this is not to suggest that critics do not appeal to various forms of authority. Nor, more important, is it to say that their sole concern is with making sense of writing which is or should be valued. As with the Tiv elders, interpretations usually come with ideological strings attached. Unfortunately these are often more difficult to recognise than an elder's sage comment or sharp put-down.

The purpose of this book is to open up some of the debate surrounding Shakespeare's *The Winter's Tale*. I will not try to stage that debate, because to do so would require that those who have contributed to it speak for themselves much more fully than space allows here. What I can do is to represent a range of critical views of the play and to suggest what is at issue between them. This means acknowledging that there is more at stake in interpretation than the exercise of reason or scholarship. All knowledge is produced, however apparently 'objective'. The facts of its production include the kinds of cultural presupposition, and even more of social and economic organisation, which enabled the Tiv to make their own sense of *Hamlet*. It follows that no act of interpretation or criticism is or ever can be wholly impartial, no critical approach ever entirely innocent. Nor is any critical approach a kind of programme of intellectual routines which can be applied to get results out of texts. Each approach has its own implications. No approach is self-contained. Even when pursuing a given approach, most critics combine methods and assumptions from others. All critics, whatever their approach(es), take much more for granted than is usually possible or convenient for them to explain.

The first half of this book aims at doing some of that explaining. Part One consists of an interrogative survey of critical approaches to *The Winter's Tale*. Its object is not to supply a digest of received opinions, handy for student or teacher, but to show both why the play is worth arguing over and the course the arguments have taken. To become aware of what different critical approaches involve or assume is a step towards greater independence. The goal is not to exercise some kind of free choice as a consumer of criticism, but to recognise what criticism entails, and so to participate more fully in making sense of all kinds of writing. To know what is at issue in competing interpretations is to be in a position not only to make choices between them, but to become capable of intervening actively for oneself.

There is a plain objection to any such survey of criticism. According to John Russell Brown, the trouble with modern Shakespeare studies is that 'It has become easier to join the critical debate than to experience the play freshly and imaginatively for oneself' (1978, p. 101). In several ways the rebuke is entirely proper. Shakespeare has been institutionalised by his importance in the school and higher educational curriculum, not to mention in the theatrical, publishing and tourist industries. Yet in one crucial sense such a complaint is naïve. It ignores the fact that no experience is immediate. It fails to admit that all understanding starts from assumptions which have already been assimilated. No mind is a tissue free for new impressions, but a collection of knowledge and habits which interact with them. Part of the purpose of this book is to lay bare some of the assumptions which underlie various kinds of understanding, so as to enable a more fully informed and constructive response. In his campaign to free Shakespeare Russell Brown also argues that it is vital to understand Shakespeare's plays as theatre. In this I wholly agree. The critical debate properly includes the special contribution of performance.

After surveying the critical debate on *The Winter's Tale* in Part One, in Part Two I offer some other ways of coming to terms with the play. Here my own views and presuppositions enter much more directly, though they are also implicit, and sometimes explicit, in the selections and judgements of Part One. I have tried to represent the views of other critics as fairly as I can, and it is right that I indicate my own standpoint. I work as a teacher in a British university, I practise no religion, and my politics are socialist. I believe that literature, like all examples of human culture, should be studied in the social and historical circumstances of its production; and that art is a form both of enjoyment and of knowledge to which all people should be entitled. These convictions, I hope, guide my work rather than bias it. One effect is in the way I present my discussion. Through its establishment in higher education the practice of criticism has tended to become unnecessarily academic. This book avoids over-specialised argument and keeps scholarly reference to a practical minimum, with the aim of opening up *The Winter's Tale* and its criticism to a wider audience.

Part One:
Survey

1 Contexts

Critical debate on *The Winter's Tale* hardly begins until the
nineteenth century. Part of the explanation for this is that by then
Shakespeare's play had long been lost to the stage. Such records
as survive suggest that the play was performed successfully for
over twenty years after its first production, but that for the next
hundred years it was not staged at all. Although revived in 1741,
in the eighteenth century it was most often performed in a series
of adaptations of which David Garrick's is known best. When most
of Shakespeare's own text was restored in 1802, with John Philip
Kemble as Leontes and Sarah Siddons as Hermione, it came as a
revelation. It is not by coincidence that critics began to take the
play more seriously soon after this date.

The chief reason why *The Winter's Tale* was so long held in low
opinion is its apparent unruliness. The play offended classically
minded critics in several ways. It mixes tragedy with comedy,
and leaves a sixteen-year gap in its action, patched over by a
curious choric speech [IV.i]. The plot is not so much improbable
as incredible, depending as it does on Hermione being long
concealed and then suddenly restored, and on Perdita not only
being saved and brought up by shepherds but being wooed by
the son of her father's former best friend. Equally bad, it seems,
Shakespeare plays fast and loose with geography and history.
He switches Sicilia and Bohemia, giving the landlocked latter a
seacoast, and, among other anachronisms, lumps together in the
same play an ancient Greek oracle with reference to the Emperor
of Russia and the sixteenth-century Italian artist Julio Romano.

Shakespeare's apparent offences against common sense and
the dramatic rules of a more critical age troubled responses to
the play less in the nineteenth than in the eighteenth century.
Part of the reason for this was the discrediting of rigid neoclassical

principles, but in retrospect the more significant point is the play's success as theatre. Garrick's version gave the first half of the play in summary, sparing his audience scenes of disturbing passion as well as what was felt as the solecism of the sixteen-year gap in the action. Its main resources were the country feast in Shakespeare's IV.iv and Hermione's restoration. Bringing most of the first half back, productions such as the one mentioned with John Philip Kemble and Sarah Siddons compelled attention to the sheer dramatic power of Leontes's mad jealousy, the responses it calls out and the effects to which it leads. This in itself, along with the acting opportunities of the part, guaranteed that the play was performed increasingly often. In addition Victorian theatre came to terms with the play's peculiarities through the opportunity it offered for spectacle. In his production of 1856 Charles Kean set the play in ancient Greece, presented in antiquarian detail that disdained no trouble or expense (Bartholomeusz, 1982, pp. 81–100). This had the best of both worlds, both spectacular and, it could be claimed, instructive, exhibiting the theatre at Syracuse and a Bacchic dance while following the eighteenth-century editor Hanmer in 'correcting' Bohemia to Bithynia.

During the nineteenth century Shakespeare's plays were dated with increasing accuracy, and critical interest in *The Winter's Tale* came to centre largely on its significance as one of his last. In a confusion of drama with autobiography, seasoned by Victorian sentiment, the themes of grace, forgiveness and reconciliation in the last plays were presented as the fruit of a serene old age. Again it was partly a revolution in performance which broke the critical mould. Granville-Barker's 1912 production, though it ran for only six weeks, is a telling example. This cast aside naïve nineteenth-century realism for a daring reliance on Shakespeare's dialogue and action. The audience was invited not to consume the play as a spectacle in a picture frame stage but, the conventional acting area broken up, to respond to it actively. John Masefield commented that the performance seemed to him 'a riper and juster piece of Shakespearian criticism' than he had ever seen in print or on stage (quoted in Pafford, 1963, p. 180); and G. Wilson Knight, a key figure in modern criticism of the last plays, has testified to the impact which Granville-Barker's productions had on him (1968, pp. 21–2, 224–5, 275–6).

It is only quite recently that the full importance of performance history to the understanding of Shakespeare's drama has become widely acknowledged in academic criticism. If, as I have been suggesting, that history properly forms one of the main contexts for Shakespearean criticism, a second main context is what has become known as 'the rise of English'. English Literature as an academic subject is largely an invention of the present century. It arose out of deep social and cultural changes which led to a slow widening of the electoral franchise and extension of educational opportunity. The history is too complex even to summarise here, but one of its main intellectual foundations was Matthew Arnold's proposal that literature might substitute for religion in a society increasingly secular. That notion found special support after the First World War as a means of promoting patriotic feeling and of displacing political questioning (see Baldick, 1983; Eagleton, 1983). Even to those critical of the Establishment, Shakespeare's work held out an image of integrated life and 'organic community' which had been lost to the present. It is in this period that the leading critics presented Shakespeare's plays as nothing less than guides to living.

A third context for criticism emerges from the growing professionalism, and professionalisation, of literary study. One way of lending credibility to English as an academic subject was to base it on established disciplines such as classics, philology and history. This move developed a life of its own in North America, where there was already a strong philological tradition, and it took on further momentum both there and in Britain as scholars and curricula gained a footing. One result was the growth of more rigorous critical attitudes. By the 1930s the critic was more likely to be a professional scholar than a cultivated gentleman. The shift towards higher standards of argument and evidence enabled great advances in knowledge. At the same time it encouraged the excessive specialisation, abstraction and forming of elites which mark criticism even more strongly today.

This brief survey of the contexts within which criticism of *The Winter's Tale* has been produced highlights three central questions. First, taking examples only from the *Casebook*, there is an argument over the play's artistic quality which runs from Ben Jonson (1631) through Dryden (1672) and Charlotte Lennox (1753) to Quiller-Couch (1918) and beyond. In *The Winter's Tale* Shakespeare almost ostentatiously defies conventionally correct style or treatment, and Jonson's gibe at his making 'Nature afraid'

(*Casebook*, p. 24) shows that this was recognised from the start. How is his dramatic unorthodoxy to be understood and judged? Second, more than most of Shakespeare's plays *The Winter's Tale* has been recommended as a kind of moral and cultural imperative, offering an image of healthy and regenerated living. Here the question is the play's relation to ideology – ideology both in its own time and in the spectator's, reader's or critic's. How far, and how explicitly, is it to be seen as a work of moral, cultural or spiritual messages; and what part if any is played by symbolism in conveying these? The third question concerns *The Winter's Tale* in study and library. It springs from the scrutiny given to the play by those who have treated it as a work with its own principles, coherence and structure, and by others who have set it in a history of ideas whose scope is not just Renaissance England but Europe. How far, if at all, should academic research determine criticism and response?

To pursue these questions is to trace much of the play's critical history, which began with evaluation and is now largely confined to the academy. In the body of Part One I will consider each kind of question in turn, before airing a number of more radical approaches which have yet to find a place in the mainstream of criticism.

2 Evaluation

Most of the earlier criticism of *The Winter's Tale* is evaluative, concerned with judging artistic merit. The first stage of critical debate on the play was dominated largely by attacks on what critics saw as the crudity of Shakespeare's technique. Extensive notes to the New Variorum edition show how the debate proceeded till the end of the nineteenth century (Furness, 1964). The case for the prosecution is conveniently put by Sir Arthur Quiller-Couch, summing up a long history of complaint (1918, pp. 287–97).

Quiller-Couch was an Edwardian gentleman of letters whose professorship in the new English School at Cambridge has been explained as 'a reward for services to the Liberal Party' (Baldick, 1983, p. 80). He approached literature as a patriotic Englishman and professional writer, hostile to theory and impatient of scholarship. Quiller-Couch accused Shakespeare of 'serious scampings

of artistry' in *The Winter's Tale* (p. 297). In particular he objected
to the suddenness of Leontes's jealousy; the seemingly awkward
transition between the first part of the play and the second; the
loss of dramatic irony in Hermione's unexpected restoration; an
apparent error over Florizel's change of clothes in IV.iv; the
handling of Antigonus's death, which he found clumsy; the lack
of any proper role for Autolycus; and, above all, Shakespeare's
failure to stage the recognition scene in V.ii between Leontes
and Perdita.

One way of challenging these objections is to accept the
analysis on which they are based but to take a different view
of Shakespeare's intentions. This is what S. L. Bethell did a
generation later (1947). Bethell's is a carefully argued Christian
interpretation which I will consider in the next section. But it
depends to a large extent on reassessing the play's technique.
This Bethell also found crude, but he suggested that the effect was
deliberate. Shakespeare had employed consciously awkward, even
archaic, dramatic methods to jolt his audience into recognising
symbolic meanings. On such a view the sequences to which
Quiller-Couch had objected become evidence of a dramatic
technique developed for presenting to sophisticated audiences
a serious religious message. Bethell also considers the play's
affronts to geography and chronology. He presents evidence to
suggest that giving Bohemia a seacoast was a contemporary joke,
and that a modern equivalent 'would be the Swiss navy or Wigan
pier' (p. 33). Similarly he points out that Julio Romano is called an
'Italian master' [V.ii.95], in other words explicitly not an artist
of the Greco-Roman period in which the play is set. The result,
Bethell argues, is that an impression is produced 'of timeless
universality' (p. 36). This is consistent with the play's other
unusual mixes, such as its presentation in IV.iv of a recognisably
English country scene, and its function is to frame a story which
is permanently valid.

A second way of answering Quiller-Couch's objections is to
reject them altogether. Nevill Coghill bases his response on a
much closer view of the play as theatre (*Casebook*, pp. 198–213). He
argues that there is nothing crude about Shakespeare's stagecraft
in *The Winter's Tale*, deliberate or otherwise. Through careful
examination of the dialogue he suggests that Leontes's jealousy
is both prepared for and motivated dramatically. Recognising
the mingled horror and grotesqueness of Antigonus's famous

exit, 'pursued by a bear' [III.iii.57], he claims that it is a theatrical masterstroke highlighting the turning point of the play. Similarly, he defends the figure of Time as central to the play's themes and suggests that only from a viewpoint of dogmatic realism could it be found redundant. He goes on to explain as natural and theatrically convincing the various moves in the 'Florizel–Perdita–Camillo–Autolycus sequence' [IV.iv.495–665], supplying stage directions which make much more sense than those of earlier editors. Lastly he appeals to the evidence of performance in arguing for the triumphant success of the two final scenes. V.ii is for him not a missed opportunity but a wonderfully adroit way of achieving a 'mounting thrill of expectation' (*Casebook*, p. 210). Most of all he denies Bethell's suggestion that the statue scene is 'stagey', claiming that its brilliant effectiveness can only be grasped when it is realised that the play is 'about a crisis in the life of Leontes, not of Hermione, and her restoration . . . is something which happens not to her, but to *him*' (p. 212). For Coghill, Shakespeare went out of his way to suggest not only that Hermione was dead but that the statue was only a statue, keeping her still and silent for maximum emotional effect both upon Leontes and the audience. He concludes: 'There is nothing antiquated or otiose in stage-craft such as this' (p. 213).

Coghill is not the only modern critic to have defended the stagecraft of *The Winter's Tale* convincingly (see Further Reading). Other writers have put different views of the sequences he discusses, but it is now widely accepted that the play is anything but crude either in construction or technique. Shakespeare is recognised as drawing freely on a variety of sources and conventions, creating a kind of dramatic collage with many-layered allusions and occasional striking counterpoint. Yet questions still remain. One of them, the role of Autolycus, I take up in Part Two. Another concerns the purpose and effects of the play's unusual methods.

Bethell proposes one answer to this, and Coghill largely accepts it even though he takes a very different view of the dramatic technique. Another alternative, however, is that the play might amount to a sophisticated tease. This view is finely expressed in Louis MacNeice's poem 'Autolycus' (*Casebook*, pp. 232-3). The poem suggests that Shakespeare himself is the arch-trickster, presenting a colourful, crowd-pulling box of 'old gags' from which

'Trinket and moral tumble out just so'. Perhaps the play is all too clever and artificial, a kind of elaborate theatrical conjuring which trades on the audience's willingness to be sentimentally if temporarily deceived. MacNeice ends up forgiving Shakespeare's 'confidence tricks'. He suggests that they were his way of coping with being 'in a fix' such as everyone has to live with. It is worth keeping in mind the humane disillusion of this perspective while considering grander or more rarefied views of the play.

3   Imagery, symbolism, myth

The final plays – *Pericles*, *Cymbeline*, *The Winter's Tale* and *The Tempest* – were first established as a group in the 1860s, but it was about seventy years before they began to attract the sustained, even reverent attention long given to Shakespeare's tragedies. One reason for this was a marked change in critical method. The dominant approach to Shakespeare studies, based largely on the tragedies, had been the character criticism which culminated in the work of A.C. Bradley (1904). In the mid-1930s this gave way to a new awareness of the importance of language and imagery. Caroline Spurgeon finds in the imagery of *The Winter's Tale* a repeated idea of 'the common flow of life through all things', likening 'human and natural processes and characteristics' (1958, pp. 305–6). She calls attention to the importance of disease imagery, and also to images of growth and development. Wolfgang Clemen approaches the role of imagery more systematically, taking account of its relation to dramatic action and of the importance not just of word painting but of visual effects on the stage. He points out the wide range of imagery in *The Winter's Tale*, and the way it works 'to create a complex, round and full picture' (1977, p. 195). That picture includes images not only from disease but from the growth and colour of the natural world, even in the play's first half; and, in the second half, images from mythology. He suggests that this blending and interweaving is apt to a play which marries court and country (pp. 203–4).

The new interest in imagery and symbolism went along with and helped stimulate another kind of approach to the last plays. In Section 1 I mentioned how, during this period, literature was often justified as a secular substitute for religion. With their emphasis on renewal and reconciliation, the last plays could be presented as offering varieties of moral and religious teaching, whether traditionally Christian or more eclectic.

Few readings of Shakespeare advance larger claims than G. Wilson Knight's. It is hardly too much to say that for him Shakespeare is the great guide to the meaning of life, the universe and everything. Though he expresses no orthodox belief, the exuberant scope of his vision has a religious force and conviction. If, as a result, his approach cannot be described as a critical method, it nevertheless follows certain principles. His usual way of discussing individual plays is to trace how the action develops, commenting sagely on its significance. From the first, even before Spurgeon and Clemen published their work, he gave special recognition to language and imagery.

The keynote for Knight's conception of *The Winter's Tale* is 'great creating Nature', the phrase which his main essay on the play takes from it [IV.iv.88] as its title. For him the play is a dramatic parable about redemption or recreation, its mystical implications given substance by plenty of vigorous, concrete imagery. Emphasising language of the natural world and its seasonal cycles, Knight speaks of the play's 'solid "world"' and '"covering sky"' as 'touchstones of reality' (1965, p. 89). There is a tension in Knight's work between inspirational vision and searching local comments. He had an active and at the time, for an academic critic, an unusual interest in theatre. Although his inclinations were towards spectacle and ritual, practical dramatic experience gave him an often shrewd insight into particulars of dialogue and action. This provides surer critical support and example than his mythmaking (and question-begging) exaltation of 'Life itself'(p. 128).

Knight finds Christian doctrine important to the play, pointing to Hermione's 'resurrection' and to Paulina as the repenting Leontes's 'conscience' (pp. 116ff., 127). He sets this, however, in a wider context of classical myth and pagan tradition. In contrast S. L. Bethell's approach is based frankly on the conviction that 'Shakespeare wrote consistently from the standpoint of orthodox Christianity' (1947, p. 14). No less than Knight does Bethell believe that the play is 'a statement, complex and profound, of the nature of reality' (p. 67; *Casebook*, p. 134). With this he couples the view of dramatic presentation mentioned earlier, in which Shakespeare's technique is seen as deliberately crude for

the purpose of focusing universal truths. The effect, for Bethell, is
to point past the limited perspectives of play and world to a reality
'beyond the possibility of illusion' (p. 57; *Casebook*, p. 125).

A second difference from Knight's approach is that Bethell's is
critically preciser. He points out, for instance, that in Hermione's
restoration Shakespeare presents 'not a genuine resurrection', but
'a carefully prepared symbol of spiritual and actual resurrection'
(p. 103). The word 'symbol' is largely the key to his method. He
distinguishes between allegory, in which there is a consistent
link between signs and meanings, and the freer imaginative
play of symbolism, 'the richer for being less explicit' (p. 75).
Shakespeare's work in general, he suggests, and *The Winter's
Tale* in particular, does not offer a message to be decoded from
a pre-established system of signs, but a creative evocation of a
meaning which language cannot directly convey. For example
Bethell argues that the characters of the last plays 'are less
important as persons than as symbols and what they are is
much less important than what they say' (p. 23). Similarly he
claims that the verse of *The Winter's Tale* is less concerned with
defining character than with inviting 'attention to themes not
explicitly stated' (p. 27).

Bethell is at pains to assert that it was not because he
was a churchman that he produced a Christian interpretation
of the play. Rather, he believes, the play expresses a Christian
vision which can be understood from a properly informed modern
perspective. Against this his approach is at times schematic, for
instance in his view that Hermione is 'life-denying' in the sense
that she submitted to 'the hermit's existence demanded by the
oracle' before Leontes's repentance (pp. 95–6). Apart from the fact
that Bethell here reads in detail where Shakespeare wisely gives
none, he fails to take into account that it is Leontes who denies
Hermione and that the image of her pregnancy is one of fertility.
More obviously tendentious is Bethell's subsequent edition of
the play (1956). This, by arguing more openly for an allegorical
reading, makes the implications of his view more explicit. One
central objection to such a reading is that, despite much careful
argument, a Christian perspective seems imposed on the play
rather than inherent in it. Another is that the word reading is,
for the most part, only too appropriate. In other words, despite
Bethell's concern for dramatic technique, his approach is from the
study not the stage. When he argues that the play's characters

are subordinate to its symbolism, or that the language points beyond their awareness, he is rarely able to indicate how the meanings he discusses could be conveyed in the theatre.

Derek Traversi's approach provides a third example of a symbolic reading. This is neither Christian, like Bethell's, nor, like Knight's, loosely anthropological. It has in common with theirs a view that the play's basic meaning is religious and that that meaning is conveyed largely through imagery. Traversi stands midway between Bethell's orthodox Christianity and Knight's unorthodoxy. Though he disclaims attempts 'to read explicit statements of Christian belief into Shakespeare', he suggests that Shakespeare produced 'a highly personal reading of that tradition' (1965, p. viii). Traversi was one of the main critics who contributed to *Scrutiny*, the most influential critical journal in England in the 1930s and 1940s. What he finds in the play is nothing less than a poetic embodiment both of rhythms in human experience which he takes to be fundamental, and of essential human values.

For Traversi, as for other *Scrutiny* critics, Shakespeare's plays are dramatic poems. Because he sees them as 'expanded images' (p. 18) the emphasis is almost exclusively on the poetry. It builds up to a sense of Shakespeare's work as a perfected whole, as if all the plays were parts of a single 'Shakespearean experience' (p. 187; *Casebook*, p. 179). Like Knight, Traversi works by tracing through the development not so much of the play's action as of themes he takes to be central. The approach is deliberate, intense, and (it is not irrelevant to add) humourless. For Traversi the themes of *The Winter's Tale* hinge on 'breakdown and reconstruction' (p. 107), a pattern in human life which, he believes, possesses the same unchanging inevitability as that of the seasons. Looking at the play in the context of Shakespeare's career, he proposes that it 'contains a profound and highly individual effort to bring the impasse suggested by Shakespeare's exploration of the part played by 'blood' in human experience – a part at once destructive and, potentially, maturing – into relation with feelings which imply the understanding of a positive spiritual conception '(pp. 119–20). This typically involved pronouncement means that Shakespeare was trying to come to terms with sex and aggression, and that he did so with the help of religion.

The values which Traversi finds central to the play are those which enable reconstruction, especially 'maturity', 'integration', and 'unity'. These are also values which he finds in the poetry, and he complains when the verse seems to him less than fully realised (e.g. p. 185; *Casebook*, p. 177). Such an approach has two dangers, of which the more obvious is that of failing to understand the play as a play. What Traversi finds to be poor poetry may be dramatically effective. In the example mentioned, for instance, he fails to recognise the possibility of humorous pathos in the Third Gentleman's elaborate language [V.ii.80-2]. The second and connected danger is over-reading, drawing more significance from a passage than can be demonstrated. For instance Traversi believes that the opening scene promises 'a gratuitous act of passion-inspired folly' which will destroy the friendship between Leontes and Polixenes (p. 108). Only someone who had read the play could be capable of such a prophecy, certainly no spectator in the theatre. Similarly he portrays the jealous Leontes as suffering 'from the same impotence of aged blood' as Polixenes later (p. 145). This is to say that senescence sets in at less than thirty.

It is possible to argue that Shakespeare's plays offer both a reading experience and a theatrical experience, and that the two are different but equally valid. Perhaps only a dramatic purist would object to such a view, but it becomes open to challenge when reading subordinates drama to essays in morality or philosophy. This is what happens especially in Bethell's and Traversi's views of *The Winter's Tale*. Traversi presents the play as a religious experience telling several essential truths about life. The trouble is that some of those 'truths' are questionable. First, Traversi speaks of 'the continuity of the family relationship, by which the father is fulfilled in his child' (p. 115). But it is an odd family relationship which lacks a mother, especially in a play in which it is women who enable redemption. Not surprisingly Traversi has little time for Paulina. Second, Traversi accepts at face value stock Elizabethan and Jacobean propaganda about monarchy. He suggests that the country's health is bound up with the king's, even to the extent that social unity 'is only conceivable under a royal guarantee' (p. 118). Yet *The Winter's Tale* presents only Leontes's court, not his country; and, as Paulina indicates, one of the dangers in a king's behaviour is tyranny. Third, and consistently with such an emphasis, Traversi insists that the kind of life presented in the pastoral scene [IV.iv] is incomplete and has to be assimilated into the courtly order for its perfection.

Again the argument is odd, for the play's structure implies that it is the court which needs to repair to the country.

Traversi, Bethell and Knight helped establish that the play was worth the fullest attention. This could not be taken for granted when it was often supposed to offer little more than romantic escape. But in doing so they over-compensated. The play became an idealised symbolic vehicle for ultimate truths about living. As Philip Edwards says in his review of criticism of the last plays, the trouble is bluntly that what is claimed as ultimate truth often turns out to be platitude (1958, pp. 11–12). In Douglas Adams's *The Hitch Hiker's Guide to the Galaxy* the computer programmed to come up with the answer to 'the great Question of Life, the Universe and Everything' produces the answer 'Forty-Two' (1979, pp. 134–5). With whatever subtlety it is carried out, the attempt to extract messages from Shakespeare produces answers which, though not absurd, are comparably reductive.

What lies behind that attempt is not so much doctrine – which even Bethell largely disclaims – as ideology. There are moments when this becomes manifest. In his edition of the play Bethell comments that 'Shakespeare had experienced the invasion of his beloved countryside by middle-class businessmen, the early stages of that urbanization of England which some people are beginning to deplore' (1956, p. 32). Although his *Study* defines an historical context for the play, this loaded remark clearly identifies part of its appeal for him. As for other critics of the time, it seems to present an image of a non-existent golden world which they believed lost. Traversi, on the other hand, severs the play from history in arguing that it conveys truths about human experience which are timeless. Yet the motives behind this are very similar, for in his reading the play becomes the symbol of an 'organic', 'integrated' (and of course royalist and patriarchal) life which no longer seems possible in the present. Similarly, Wilson Knight's jargon reveals his standpoint when he says that 'the crown is always to be understood as a symbol piercing the eternity dimension' (1965, p. 107; *Casebook*, p. 145). Such emphases are matter for debate. Nevertheless, with their work on the play's imagery, and their speculations on its symbolic possibilities, Knight, Bethell, Traversi and others helped bring into focus the importance of its verse and poetic language. This is probably their main legacy to criticism of the last plays.

4 Allegory and theme

Bethell's *Study* of *The Winter's Tale* avoids treating the play as an allegory, though his edition, with its pointers towards Shakespeare's 'inner meaning', is less restrained (1956, e.g. pp. 33–40). Others go much further. Though most contribute little to the debate on the play, they illustrate a great deal about the practice of criticism.

J. A. Bryant pushes a Christian reading to – or beyond – the limit. Not only does he present the play as an allegory of mankind's redemption, but he fits in all the main characters neatly. Leontes and Mamillius between them stand for Judaism, Polixenes for the Gentiles, and Paulina for St Paul; while Hermione, it is easy to guess, is 'a type of the Christ' (1955, p. 214). Glynne Wickham takes a different approach entirely. He proposes that '*The Winter's Tale* represents Shakespeare's contribution to the celebrations marking the investiture of Henry Stuart as Prince of Wales and heir apparent to the reunited Kingdoms of England, Wales and Scotland in June 1610' (1973, p. 88). Wickham claims that he reads the play as emblem rather than allegory, since the parallels he proposes between dramatic action and historical events are incomplete. But in practice there is little difference. For instance, Wickham suggests that Leontes is to be viewed as three characters: himself at narrative level; in the first part of the play as the mythical Brutus who divided England (Sicilia) from Scotland (Bohemia); and in Act V as the second Brutus, James I, who reunited the kingdom. Similarly Hermione is to be seen as Britain, 'the wife divorced by the first Brutus and mystically restored to the second', and Perdita as 'Reunited Britannia' (p. 97). Wickham caps the whole conceit by supposing that Paulina stands for Francis Bacon and that the Third Gentleman in V.ii might have been played by Shakespeare himself.

These two examples are representative in several ways. First, they indicate two of the commonest kinds of allegorical interpretation in Shakespeare criticism: the religious, and especially Christian; and the occasional, invoking contemporary events. Second, both are put forward in all seriousness and were taken seriously enough to be printed in reputable publications. A third characteristic is the means by which they claimed scholarly attention. Although both interpretations are at the very least strained, both do much to muster academic credibility. Bryant

advances a set of theological and literary precedents; he simply
fails to establish any link with *The Winter's Tale*. Wickham gives
much more historical detail, but also argues for the existence of
an emblematic tradition not only in the art of the period but its
drama. This interesting line of enquiry only gets stretched too
thin when he uses it as a lassoo for Shakespeare's play.

Both essays are exhibits for the prosecution in Richard
Levin's attack on allegorical and thematic interpretations of
Shakespeare. Levin points out that 'it is very easy to work out
some kind of allegory for *any* play (or any narrative)' (1980, p. 3).
Substantiating it is much more difficult, and Levin shows why by
presenting at length both negative and positive evidence. On the
one hand there are no records indicating that any contemporary
of Shakespeare's ever saw in *The Winter's Tale* an allegory of any
sort. On the other hand there is strong evidence for the grounds
on which performed plays actually were valued. These are in particular 'for the portrayal of intrinsically interesting personalities
and their actions' (p. 10); for 'the success of these characters and
actions in creating the illusion of reality and in engaging the
emotions of the audience' (p. 11); and for the actors' ability to
convince the audience 'that their actions were "real"', and so to
arouse 'the audience's feelings, especially feelings of compassion
for the characters they portrayed' (p. 14). Levin concludes that
either the critics 'are wrong in claiming that [Shakespeare's]
plays were meant to convey allegories, or, if they are right,
these plays were failures, since the people for whom they were
written did not find, and presumably did not even look for, any
allegories in them' (p. 23). All of which seems to indicate that the
best guide for approaching Shakespeare is plain, literal minded,
commonsense.

Levin's powerful case is worth testing against a more cogent
interpretation. Alastair Fowler's reading of *The Winter's Tale* avoids
Bryant's simplification and Wickham's academic fancy. Instead,
it weaves together a number of motifs drawn from the history
of ideas, and − more to the point − applies them to problems
other critics have found in the play. Fowler suggests that the
play's subject is less the jealousy of Leontes than what it leads
to, 'the difficulty of repentance' (1978, p. 37). He bases his
argument on a mixture of Renaissance mythology, Christian
doctrine and various symbolic schemes of the period, involving
especially numbers, flowers and the ages of man. His discussion

of Hermione's role will serve to illustrate his approach and outline his findings. The name, Fowler points out, is not in Shakespeare's source, *Pandosto*, and in the Renaissance it was confused creatively with Harmonia. So, he claims, what Leontes loses in his rage is nothing less than the soul's harmony. But the highlight of Fowler's interpretation is his account of Hermione's mysterious disappearance and restoration, problems for many critics of the play. He disdains any suggestion that Paulina deliberately stage-manages these, waiting till Leontes is worthy of Hermione again. Instead, he proposes, Hermione vanishes because Leontes is spiritually dead until he can repent: 'It is as if he repented only intellectually or formally in Act III' (p. 50). Then the statue does not so much come to life as respond to what happens in Leontes: 'the movable statue signifies a potentiality of repentant emotion' (p. 52). Fowler further suggests that 'Hermione turned statue may be soul restored by art' (p. 54). His dense, ingenious and learned essay contains much else of interest which there is no space to summarise here. The question is whether any of it will survive Levin's devastating attack on all allegorical readings of Shakespeare's plays.

The best place to begin for an answer is with those features of *The Winter's Tale* which seem to encourage allegorical interpretation. First, critics have often argued that characterisation in the last plays is less full and detailed than in most of Shakespeare's earlier work, especially the tragedies which immediately preceded them. The contrast most often cited is between Leontes and Othello. If this is so – and the point should not be accepted without question – it is possible to suggest that characters in the last plays are not only significant in themselves but carry various symbolic meanings. Second, the action of the last plays involves the mysterious and supernatural. In *The Winter's Tale*, for example, there is the oracle of Apollo, the saving of Perdita, the destruction of 'all the instruments which aided to expose the child' [v.ii.69], and of course Hermione's disappearance and restoration. Such action, it may be claimed, can only be understood in terms of religious faith. Third, the rich, complex language of the last plays, especially of *The Winter's Tale*, may be read as conveying symbolic suggestions. Fowler, for instance, draws attention to 'the play's many universalizing speeches with religious overtones' (p. 39), and to the religious language surrounding Hermione's restoration (p. 52). Finally, critics have pointed to elements of masque in the last plays. Masques enjoyed popularity at Court in this period and were often explicitly allegorical. It is not implausible that Shakespeare exploited the qualities of masque for meaning as well as decoration.

Although he does not say so, the reason why Levin does not take into account these qualities of the play is that he aims to cut out the ground beneath any allegorical reading of Shakespeare whatsoever. Where he convinces fully is in rebutting interpretations like Bryant's and Wickham's which rely on a single (and unlikely) set of links. It is more difficult to dispose of a reading like Fowler's which presents the play not as offering a rigid external meaning but as intimations of symbolic possibility. Here the special qualities of the last plays have a right for consideration; though I emphasise that the nature of these is itself subject to debate. Levin is too absolute in one way as critics like Bryant and Wickham are in another. Although none of Fowler's claims can be proved, none of Levin's evidence destroys them.

The same principle becomes clearer when Levin goes on to attack thematic as well as allegorical interpretation. A theme in a literary work is an idea abstracted from it. As Levin correctly says, it follows that to represent a particular theme as conveying the essential meaning of a work is 'a less extreme form of allegorical criticism' (p. 23). Levin has devoted a book as well as the article I have been discussing to the problem of such 'new readings' (1979). He is certainly right in pointing out that a major stimulus behind these is the pressure on academics to publish. It is also true that a moral or philosophical theme has the attraction, specious though it may be, of looking more impressive intellectually. So there is much to be said for Levin's attempt to redirect critics to the primary human events of the plays. Yet in two ways he overstates his case. First, thematic readings based on old favourites like appearance and reality, reason and passion, or order and chaos can still be culled from bibliographies, but they are not now taken very seriously. Second, few thematic readings now present absolute claims. It is one thing to argue that a particular theme unlocks the whole meaning of a play. It is quite another to suggest that knowledge of Elizabethan or Jacobean thinking about a theme which is prominent in the play is both relevant and contributes properly to its understanding. This second, much more defensible, path is the one most often taken today. I will end this section with two examples. Neither, incidentally, is mentioned by Levin.

E. W. Tayler argues that the theme of nature versus art occupied Shakespeare throughout his career, but that it became 'a vital and living problem for him in the ethical speculations of the last plays' (1964, p. 125), especially *The Winter's Tale*. He begins by presenting the pastoral scene [IV.iv] as central to the play, reflecting the harmony with which it began and offering a 'structural and symbolic prelude to the restoration of harmony in the last act' (p. 133). Similarly he suggests that central to that scene is the argument between Perdita and Polixenes about the relationship of Nature and Art [IV.iv. 79–103]. He makes three main points. First, the positions taken by both characters are traditional and 'philosophically "respectable"' (p. 137); Shakespeare was drawing on a long-established debate. Second, those positions are apt dramatically. As a king, it is proper for Polixenes to state the case for Art, associated as it was with courtly sophistication. Equally Perdita's challenge comes out of a robust simplicity and freedom from hypocrisy associated with the country. In one way both reason against their own position, for in social terms a marriage between Perdita and Florizel would constitute just such a mixture as they debate. Yet, by a further irony, both are right in different ways. Perdita's 'nature', as the audience will be aware, actually is royal. So, though he means it in a different sense, Polixenes is doubly right to say that 'The art itself is Nature' [IV.iv.97]. Lastly, having teased out these paradoxes, Tayler applies them to the closing scene. Again, as with Perdita, 'the imitation or "mock" of Nature turns out finally to be Nature after all. What seems to be Art is in fact Nature, fulfilling Polixenes' assertion that the "art itself is nature" and confirming Perdita's belief in the supremacy of "great creating nature"' (p. 140). So the earlier argument about the relative claims of nature and art is transcended.

Tayler adds an interesting note on a contemporary treatment of the same theme. In comparison with Spenser, he suggests, 'Shakespeare thinks *about* the terms [of the debate] more than he does *with* them . . . perhaps because of his lack of absolute commitment he can afford to extract from various and conflicting interpretations the full dramatic value of the philosophical division' (p. 141). This is an important reminder of how fully, in Shakespeare, philosophical issues are subordinate to drama.

It also demonstrates proper critical scruple in not claiming too much for a theme. Where Tayler's argument might be questioned is in his too ready acceptance of a courtly bias to the debate. When he declares that 'Perdita's royal blood manifests itself despite her surroundings and not because of them' (p. 133), he fails to allow for the kindness, warmth and hospitality which characterise her life with the shepherds. It is not surprising that an academic critic should take the part of established culture. Polixenes and Autolycus also patronise the shepherds, but the play lets neither get away with it.

A second constructive example of a thematic reading is Inga-Stina Ewbank's essay on Time. Again the approach is to consider an issue which, in the context of the history of ideas, has clear and central importance in the play. Ewbank points out that Renaissance iconography portrayed Time in two aspects, both Destroyer and Revealer. The division corresponds to the two parts of the play, and also suits the marked change of dramatic rhythm from the 'hectic effect' of the first part, with its plunging forward movement, to the 'leisurely pace' especially of the long pastoral scene (*Casebook*, pp. 102, 109). It is marked, too, by the arrival of Time himself as a character on the stage. This Ewbank vigorously and rightly defends. For her, Time is no mere 'programme note', but a 'pivotal image, part verbal part visual, of the Triumph of Time. . . . Shakespeare presses home the fact that the "wide gap" of dramatically "untried growth" is part of the universal process of time who "makes and unfolds error" in his immutable onward flight' (p. 105). Like Tayler, Ewbank also helps illuminate the pastoral scene. Not only is time here presented as equivalent to 'the life of nature and the cycle of the seasons', as shown by Perdita's flower-speeches and flower-giving (p. 108). There is also an awareness, especially in Perdita and confirmed by Polixenes's outburst, that change and death threaten in Arcadia too. Ewbank then demonstrates how, the threat overcome, Perdita and Florizel remove another danger, through that means of defeating time represented by healthy offspring.

Ewbank ends her essay by emphasising that *The Winter's Tale* is not a 'treatise on time': 'The play does not state or prove anything' (p. 114). Nevertheless she tends on occasion to exaggerate the importance of the theme in something of the manner deplored by Levin. This is not so much by her claim that the triumph of time is 'a controlling theme' of the play (p. 99), as by her emphasis on time as an independent agent. It is misleadingly abstract to propose that the play shows 'what time does to man' (pp. 99, 114), when the stage action presents what man does to man – and especially woman. Ewbank's reading tends to imply a cycle of events which has a timeless inevitability. This minimises not only Leontes's guilt but the courageous and principled stand of Hermione – whom Ewbank links rather schematically with Justice (p. 103). It is fair to conclude that, although Tayler and Ewbank add to the play's understanding, Levin's caution is justified. It is a mistake to lose sight of the primary human situations.

5 Genre and convention

As there are several strong similarities between the last plays they are often considered as a group, separate in various ways from the rest of Shakespeare's work. Some have traced the change of direction to developments in Jacobean theatre, especially the popularity of the masque and the move towards smaller, indoor acting areas. Both factors may have had their influence, though Shakespeare's company continued to stage plays at the Globe and the element of masque is easily over-emphasised.

Another way of understanding the last plays as a group is to study them in terms of a common structure and set of conventions. This is known as 'generic criticism', after the French term 'genre' or 'kind'. According to a theory which goes back to Aristotle and was taken very seriously at least until the eighteenth century, each literary kind has its own laws and conventions; so that, for instance, certain types of character, situation, or behaviour are proper to comedy and other types to tragedy. Northrop Frye has written widely and influentially in this field. His work is of special interest because much of it centres on Shakespearean comedy and romance.

All Frye's writing is part of a grand general theory about the nature and function of literature (1957). He believes that literature is descended from ritual and magic, and conventions from myths. The fundamental myth, for Frye, is one of death and rebirth. This is patterned on the cycle of the seasons, with each of which he associates one of the main literary kinds: comedy with spring, summer with romance, autumn with tragedy and winter with satire. It is also represented by Christianity, which for Frye is the most comprehensive myth of all. Frye identifies *The Winter's Tale* as a romance, a genre he defines as offering a golden, paradisal world of wish-fulfilment. The romance has a long history stretching back to ancient Greece, and the form it takes can be narrative as well as dramatic, as in *Pandosto*, the source of Shakespeare's play. In Frye's account *The Winter's Tale* is a diptych, a display with two sides, in which the cruel power of winter gives way to summer's health and healing (*Casebook*, pp.184–97). The keynote of the first half is Mamillius's ghost story [II.i.25–30], so abruptly broken off; of the second half Autolycus's song [IV.iii.1–22] of spring and coming summer (1965, p. 155). Frye also finds in the play overtones of Christian myth, from the suggestions of sacrifice (Mamillius, Antigonus, the mariners), to Hermione's miraculous restoration.

This summary may suggest that Frye's approach combines Wilson Knight's with S. L. Bethell's, but there are several important differences. Frye shares with Knight an approach to literature as myth, and with Bethell a commitment to Christianity. Like the latter he also studied theology, and became an ordained minister as Bethell did not. What most distinguishes his approach from Knight's and Bethell's is that he claims a properly scientific basis and method. For him literature is to be studied as a self-contained system, to which value judgements and any reference to the real world are irrelevant. So, unlike Bethell, he refuses to claim any symbolic or allegorical dimension for *The Winter's Tale*: 'the meaning of the play is the play' (1965, p. 116). Similarly he denies any view of Shakespeare as a kind of poetic guru. For him the last plays do not represent a supreme, mature wisdom, as they do for Knight or Traversi, so much as 'the end of the steady growth of Shakespeare's technical interest in the structure of drama' (p. 8). It follows that 'Shakespeare had no opinions, no values, no philosophy, no principles of anything except dramatic structure' (p. 39). So much for the idea of the writer as philosopher and prophet.

Frye's criticism has stimulated the study of comedy and increased awareness of structural similarities between works of often widely different types. But it is open to several objections. The most formidable of these is that the theory and its practice are reductive. This applies less to the pigeonholing of various works, because Frye's own criticism is sensitive to all sorts of shadings and distinctions, than to what the theory leaves out. The most massive omission is history, for Frye disregards the rootedness of literature in specific times and places, its ability to respond to particular questions and pressures. Hardly less serious is the diminishing both of the writer's and of the reader's relation to the work. This is especially inappropriate to a performance art like drama, based as it is on interaction between play and audience. Frye's breezy dismissals of everything but the literary stem from his basic assumption that literature is a self-contained system. Yet the emergence of that assumption is to be explained according not to logic but to history. The attempt at producing a scientific theory of literature should be seen in its cultural and historical setting, when a growing critical profession was seeking to establish intellectual territory and prestige, and when literature seemed to offer a supplement or even a replacement to fading systems of religion and morality (Eagleton, 1983).

Other approaches to *The Winter's Tale* as a play of a particular kind have sprung more directly from a tradition of scholarship than Frye's. Joan Hartwig, for instance, has suggested that the play is an example of tragicomedy rather than of romance. This extends what is already implied by the image of the diptych, applied to the play by Frye as well as by others, in which a 'tragic' development is followed by a 'comic' resolution. But Hartwig goes further by arguing that *The Winter's Tale* is of mixed kind throughout. She draws attention to comic elements in the first, 'tragic', part of the play, such as the exchanges between Paulina and Leontes in II. iii; and to the effect in the second, 'comic', part of Autolycus's 'decadent complexity' (1972, pp. 117–18). She also suggests that such a mixture is consistent not only with Renaissance theory of tragicomedy, but with the mongrel tendencies of native British tradition.

On the one hand Hartwig offers 'The Exploration of a Genre', as the title of her first chapter describes it. This is linked, however, with what she calls a 'rhetorical' approach to the last plays (p. 9). The problem she sets herself is that of 'educating our responses so that they are adequate for the drama Shakespeare has given us' (p. 175). What results is a less schematic criticism than Frye's, one more attentive to the tone and detail of dramatic interplay as well as to literary history. Hartwig is careful to insist on the rashness of supposing that 'Shakespeare should have limited himself to any given pattern' (p. 12), but suggests instead a highly self-conscious mastery of genre and convention for essentially moral purposes. In other words from an academic perspective she develops a view of the last plays which, with certain qualifications, finds in them the same kind of hope and example as is celebrated by Knight, Bethell and Traversi. Like Bethell Hartwig is especially interesting on the play's deliberate artifice. Where she is less convincing is in expressing what this leads to, as when she concludes: 'Shakespeare's tragicomic mode renews man's world by educating the characters' powers to see and to understand meaning beyond their own narrow limits' (p. 178). So vague a summing up disappoints after the closely argued criticism before.

As Hartwig points out, the danger of the approach through genre or convention lies in imposing a sort of critical straitjacket. It may be that one work or another does not so much conform to convention as play with it or put it in question. A parallel danger in Hartwig's 'rhetorical' criticism lies in attributing responses to the audience. This is always a dubious exercise, as it takes for granted the nature not only of that audience but of production and performance. No one of these is ever either single or stable, so differences and even conflicts in response will always occur. Perhaps because she is sensitive to the problem Hartwig draws back from an opportunity her own approach creates – that of arguing that the last plays set out to educate not so much the characters but the audience 'to see and to understand meaning beyond their own narrow limits'. The history of ideas enables such a possibility to be explored at least for a Renaissance audience. This is an approach which depends on research into ways of thinking and seeing characteristic of a given period. It offers to reconstruct the assumptions which artists and contemporaries brought to works of art, both in making them and in responding to them.

Rosalie L. Colie is one of those who have discussed what kind of play *The Winter's Tale* is through the history of ideas. Her manifesto is uncompromising: 'Whatever the critical arguments against generic studies in our time . . . I know that *not* to be aware of generic boundaries, generic definitions, generic models is, at the very least, to make much of Renaissance literature altogether unintelligible' (1974, p. 27). The problem with this claim is not only that it is totalitarian, but that the argument on which it is based is circular. The intelligibility of Renaissance writing is defined in terms of meanings limited by the history of genre. In practice, though, Colie can be more flexible. She recognises that Shakespeare 'of all authors seems freest in breaking patterns' (p. 11), and her discussion of *The Winter's Tale* amply demonstrates the point.

Colie begins with *As You Like It*, written about twelve years before *The Winter's Tale*. This she presents as a perfect fulfilment of the creative opportunities provided by pastoral comedy. Then she shows how *The Winter's Tale* turns the same conventions upside down and inside out. The crux of her argument is that Shakespeare 'did not *have* to write this way; he obviously chose to conduct a frontal examination of the structural and thematic limits of modern pastoral drama, that is, of tragicomedy'. As a result, she argues, the play 'simply forces us to face what is "tragic" and what "comic" in life and in plays, forces questions of genre and decorum' (p. 267). Shakespeare goes beyond genre and convention in *The Winter's Tale* with breathtaking freedom, suggesting not only that 'art is not what it seems' but that 'life is not what it seems either' (p. 283). This might be taken to imply that study of genre and convention is of limited use with Shakespeare. But Colie would no doubt answer that his plays are properly understood only by recognising what conventions he worked with, even – perhaps especially – when he left them behind.

Most of the recent academic criticism on the last plays in general and *The Winter's Tale* in particular has focused on this kind of question. One danger in the approach lies in assuming, with Frye, that literature is made almost exclusively out of literature. Another danger, as references and footnotes proliferate, is that criticism seems increasingly to be made out of criticism. Approaching *The Winter's Tale* as a genre critic, Colie speaks of Hermione's 'genre preferences' and says that Leontes finally has to 'submit to the romance conventions' (p. 270). This is playful if ponderous wit, but the danger of pressing such an approach becomes clearer when Robert Uphaus declares that the play's major issue, 'for both the characters and the audience, settles down to a contest between the forces and conventions of tragedy . . . and the evolution and development of romance' (1981, p. 76). The major issue for the 'generic critic', that is.

This kind of academic sophistry can be avoided, but a central critical problem remains for all studies of the last plays as a group. This is simply that, for all the similarities between them, there are also important differences. Indeed some of the differences look highly deliberate: according to the humorous categories Shakespeare gave to Polonius in *Hamlet*, *The Winter's Tale* is a 'poem unlimited', while *The Tempest*, with its time, place and action carefully circumscribed, presents a 'scene individable' [II.ii.395–6]. It is as if Shakespeare was showing what he could do at both ends of the dramatic spectrum. Stanley Wells gives a further useful caution. Not only is the word 'romance' unknown in Shakespeare's writings, but it seems never to have been used to describe a play at the period (1966, p. 49). More important, *The Winter's Tale* is uncharacteristic of romance in its 'emphasis on personal responsibility', as with Leontes's guilt for his son's death (p. 66). This suggests again that with Shakespeare reasoning from the general, or the generic, is not enough.

6   Structure and source

One way to avoid the danger of dissolving text in assumed context is to focus on those qualities which make the text unique. Its particular style and language deserve the closest attention. So too does the structure of the work, the way it is put together. This appears to offer a more objective understanding, in the sense that the work is studied in terms of its own articulation. Structure can be demonstrated by analysis, and does not seem subject to such judgements or assumptions as are required by arguments based on convention or symbolic scheme. So Fitzroy Pyle, one of those who deal with the structure of the play, compares himself not to the Mr Interpreter of Bunyan's *Pilgrim's Progress* but to 'Mr. Spectator the impartial observer seeking to record what is there for him to see' (1969, p. xi). In assessing the value of the approach it is worth asking how far this claim is justified.

Ernest Schanzer has suggested that *Pericles* provides the 'structural model' for *The Winter's Tale*, in that alone among Shakespeare's plays the two possess a 'double focus' (*Casebook*, p. 87). The subjects of this focus are a father and a daughter. In both plays the first three acts centre on the father; the fourth act, in which he does not appear at all, on the daughter; and the last on the family's reunion. Both also pivot on a long time-lapse, sharpening the contrasts between the two parts of the play it divides.

Schanzer points out that in developing the pattern first laid down in *Pericles* Shakespeare created an extensive network of parallels and contrasts. He distinguishes four main kinds (p. 96). There are 'structural parallels', such as the brief prose scene which introduces each of the play's two parts [I.i. and IV.ii]; 'thematic parallels', like the shattering outburst of Leontes in II.i and of Polixenes in IV.iv; 'plot-parallels', such as Camillo helping both Polixenes and Florizel against royal threat; and finally 'parallels of tone and atmosphere', such as that between the reverent description of the oracle [III.i] and the statue scene [V.iii]. Schanzer does not present these categories as wholly separate, and the distinction between 'thematic' and 'plot' parallels might be questioned. Clearly, however, a pattern of repetition exists and one of its functions is to divide and then reconnect the play's two parts. For Schanzer, Autolycus's line 'the red blood reigns in the winter's pale' [IV.iii.4] 'sums up the basic progression of the play' (p. 90). Time inverts his hour glass to mark the sixteen years between the two parts, balancing and reversing the trial scene of III.ii with the statue scene. This basic design is inlaid by complementary patterns in the imagery. On the one hand, Schanzer suggests, there are contrasts between 'images of planting and growth with images of uprooting and blight, and . . . images of health and physic with images of sickness and infection' (p. 94). On the other hand, the second part not only sets 'the creative, fertile, and natural against the destructive, barren, and monstrous' (p. 95), but replaces pastoral imagery early in the play with actual shepherds and a pastoral scene.

In his analysis Schanzer provides quite a large number of detailed examples, but the conclusions he draws are fairly modest. Pointing out that the effect of the play's parallels and contrasts is on the whole not ironic, he suggests that instead recurrence helps universalise the action. For him the result 'is to increase our sense of the fragility, the precariousness of human happiness', evoking an affinity 'between human affairs and the cycle of the seasons' (p. 97).

Slightly shortened and revised, Schanzer's essay forms part of his introduction to the Penguin edition of the play. Here he goes further to consider another aspect of the play's construction, its relation to the undisputed primary source. Shakespeare took his plot for *The Winter's Tale* from Robert Greene's narrative romance *Pandosto*, first published in 1588 and popular until the eighteenth century. Schanzer defines two major and several minor changes. First is Shakespeare's restoration of Hermione, in contrast to *Pandosto* where the queen stays dead. Second is the way in which Perdita is abandoned, which Shakespeare made 'not only more suited to the stage but also more credible' (1969, p. 16). Among the minor changes are altered names, the transposition of Bohemia and Sicilia, and the creation of several new characters, especially Antigonus, Paulina and Autolycus. Schanzer also calls attention to Shakespeare's transformation of the story's central figures. The result, he suggests, is not only much more convincing but also more sympathetic characterisation, especially of Leontes, Florizel and Perdita. Characterisation in romance is typically thin and conventional, and it is often held that Shakespeare provides no exception. But Schanzer roundly declares that 'there is nothing that marks off Shakespeare's treatment of characters in *The Winter's Tale* from that in his mature comedies and tragedies' (p. 28).

Schanzer argues that the principal effect of these changes is 'to bring the play closer to the world of Greek romance' (p. 16). Though this follows from the evidence he gives, especially the 'rousing of a feeling of wonder' in Hermione's restoration, the emphasis is odd. It is as if Schanzer were trying to establish Shakespeare's scholarly credentials, contesting the once common view that the play is clumsy and artless. But the cost is to leave out of account what in the play is characteristically Elizabethan and Jacobean. Shakespeare's version of the pastoral scene is English and his own, whatever its sources and allusions. And, as I will suggest later, the social and political questions raised by the play are not simply literary or conventional. Study of the structure of a work or its relation to a source is less objective than it may appear. Given the existence of structural patterns – and even these are subject to definition – there is more than one way of understanding their effect. Given a relation between text and source, there is more than one way of interpreting it. One example is the way Schanzer ranks Shakespeare's changes. Among these Hermione's restoration is certainly crucial. But little less important is the creation of Paulina, for whom there is no equivalent whatever in the source, and who plays a vital role as Hermione's defender. Other signs of Schanzer's position are his special pleading for Antigonus (p. 18) and for the court (p. 44), and the grudging view he takes of Perdita's upbringing in the country (pp. 43–4). Such emphases are at least arguable, and certainly not neutral ideologically. They suggest an endorsement of patriarchal values, hierarchy and courtly sophistication which is not self-evident in the play. Shakespeare is sometimes claimed as a cultural conservative, and this is a proper topic for debate. It is also proper to recognise, and question, any implicit ideological claim.

Fitzroy Pyle, as already mentioned, disavows any other aim than detailed textual study. With its close attention to *Pandosto*, his scene-by-scene commentary offers 'an experience of the play as a transmutation of its primary source' (pp. x–xi). The result is a celebration of Shakespeare's craftsmanship as he sees it. Pyle contributes many astute local comments. He suggests, for instance, the importance of IV.iii not only in the surprise effect of Autolycus and his amoral message of spring, but in enabling 'the sheep-shearing scene to begin without preliminaries' (p. 78). Similarly he argues that V.i, in which Leontes welcomes the unexpected Florizel and Perdita, has the effect of a recognition scene even though Leontes does not know Perdita's true identity (p. 106). This disables the complaint that Shakespeare failed to stage a scene of such importance, and Pyle follows up by pointing to what he achieved in V.ii with its mounting excitement and ironic surprises. He goes on to deal convincingly with Shakespeare's artistry in the statue scene. This shows the advantage of his approach, in that it enables him to draw out complexities to which more schematic criticism is blind. Pyle quotes Northrop Frye's comment that the audience is not to inquire further about Hermione's restoration, fantastic as it seems. The point is in keeping with Frye's emphasis both on acceptance of literary convention and on what he sees as the need in this sequence for religious or quasi-religious belief. But Pyle rightly adds that Shakespeare does not leave it at that; as soon as Hermione speaks 'we have entered the realm of factual explanation' (p. 132). His own view does fuller justice to the scene. It has, he argues,

> two parts, mystification and resolution, one passing into the other in the lines that separate Hermione's revival from her recovering the power of speech. While the stage magic

of the statue engrosses us our critical faculties are dormant. As the sense of wonder fades they start working again, and Shakespeare seeks to satisfy (or appear to satisfy) our scruples, even the most mundane. (p. 132)

As these examples suggest, Pyle treats the play as an experience in the theatre. But he does not refer to any evidence from performance, and without this such an approach is difficult to sustain. Although he correctly insists on the irrelevance of questions which could not arise in production (e.g. p. 73), some of his own speculations seem tied to an idea of the staging which is based more on imagination than practice. Despite, for instance, a perceptive discussion of the dramatic pacing in the first three scenes (pp. 30–1), he oddly insists that Hermione should not be shown as pregnant. For him only verbal rather than visual notice is necessary (pp. 16–17), though such modesty would be sure to reduce the dramatic impact and the impression of Hermione's femininity. Second, Pyle believes that the play has a five-act structure, so the action should properly pause at the main divisions. However, although the copy text for the play in the 1623 Folio has act and scene divisions, these are almost certainly not Shakespeare's. The evidence suggests that he wrote his plays to be performed without a break (see e.g. Hirsh, 1981). On the assumption that *The Winter's Tale* is constructed in five acts Pyle objects to the numbering of IV.i (p. 76). For him it spoils the symmetry between I.i and IV.ii, which are parallel both as prose scenes and in other ways. But this is a nicety which could scarcely be noticed in the theatre.

Pyle's comments on Autolycus further illustrate his method. Approaching the play from its source, he proposes a formal reason for the character's invention. This is that Shakespeare's development of Camillo unfitted him for part of the role of his original, Capnio, so that another character, also suitably developed, had to take on that part instead (pp. 165–6). Pyle suggests that beyond his contribution to the plot Autolycus is chiefly a source of highly enjoyable entertainment – young, to contrast with Camillo, and a fine singer and jester. He believes, for instance, that in V.ii Autolycus stays true to form by picking pockets. This is not only a cliché of the scene, but, as I will argue later, in other ways out of place. There is more of an edge to Autolycus than the role of 'stage thief' (p. 79) permits.

The view Pyle takes of Shakespeare's methods of construction is literary rather than dramatic, and his approach is also literary in another sense. In honouring Shakespeare's craftsmanship he certainly avoids the large and often excessive claims advanced by those who press thematic, allegorical or symbolic readings. But though his approach shows an attractive modesty, it tends to abstract the play from the real world, leaving it as an artefact, beautiful but self-contained. It is revealing that Pyle defines the essential theme both of the last plays and of *King Lear* as 'family unity – suffering and loss in the family, the inseparably related fortunes of two generations' (p. 190). That theme is certainly central, but it could not be guessed from Pyle's account that all five plays also raise political questions. Against this Pyle would probably argue that *The Winter's Tale* is in touch with the real world in that it bears out what he calls 'the full statement of reality . . . life *and* death, static fact *and* mobile potentiality' (p. 149). But this depends on defining 'the real world' in terms so general as to exclude much human experience, including the realities of life and death when these lie within the power of others. The working of the eternal verities often turns out to be highly contingent.

The basis of the approaches taken by Schanzer and Pyle is formal or aesthetic. They treat the play as an artefact, with its own form and being. Yet, as I have tried to show, even these apparently objective readings, scrupulous as they are, carry ideological emphases. In the next three sections I will consider approaches to the play which, avoiding the illusion of objectivity, wear their theoretical or ideological preferences on their sleeves.

7 Marxism

Those who approach Shakespeare from a Marxist perspective try to restore what in many critical accounts goes missing: an understanding of the plays within the social and historical processes in which they were written and acted. History of ideas, study of genre and convention, various allegorical interpretations – all these set up historical contexts of a sort. But what Marxist critics claim to offer is an understanding of the conditions which determine the way works of art are made. Marx never assembled his writings on art into a coherent theory, and Marxist theory continues to develop, so there are many different kinds of Marxist approach. Charles Barber's essay on *The Winter's Tale* provides a single example.

Barber begins by suggesting 'that the play is more directly concerned with the problems of Jacobean society than is usually recognized' (1964, p. 233). As this might seem odd to those who view the play as a sophisticated fairy-tale, or a myth, he deals with both objections. Agreeing that the play is not naturalistic, he points out that this does not mean it is remote from reality. And he quickly demonstrates from the dramatic language how firm is its grasp of human experience. Similarly he discounts the approach to the play as myth. Despite its religious symbolism, he suggests, it contains too much 'rich and immediate human experience' to fit any neat symbolic scheme (p. 237). Instead, Barber proposes, the play's key theme is 'the contrast and conflict between court and country'. This provides the structure of the play, in a movement from court to countryside and back again, setting up 'a kind of thesis-antithesis-synthesis pattern'. The court, he argues, is presented as needing renewal from the country. First, it is 'the source of passion which leads to tyranny' (p. 238). This is borne out by the furious intemperance both of Leontes and Polixenes. Second, 'the court is shown as being in danger of spinelessness and of over-artificiality' (p. 241). Barber finds the courtiers ineffectual in their attempts to restrain Leontes, and effete in their conversation – as in the opening and penultimate scenes. In contrast, 'the cottage is the source of humanity and of naturalness' (p. 243). Not only is the language refreshingly down to earth, but the Shepherd is one of nature's gentlemen and his home a centre of hospitality. The opposition of court and country is reconciled through Perdita and Florizel. One has been cast from the court on the country's mercy, the other has sought the country, turning his back on the court. Both return from where they came, taking Perdita's substitute family with them. This Barber reads as offering 'a reconciliation between court and country, in which renewal will be brought to the court from below, while the inhabitants of the cottage will be refined by the influence of the court' (p. 244).

Two of the possible objections to this reading Barber meets head on. The fact of Perdita's royalty he turns round, as a let-out 'for the courtiers in the audience who need it'. Similarly he agrees that the tone of several sequences involving the Shepherd and Clown is farcical; but he denies that this diminishes their humanity. Barber is one of the few critics who refuse to patronise the country characters, and for him their elevation is accepted by the play 'with good humour and equanimity' (p. 245). Further, he does not intellectualise the theme of Art versus Nature, but sets it in a wider context of 'man's control of nature'. This is shown in the play's imagery, and it is connected with the emphasis on the basic realities of life in the country. Similarly Barber suggests, again largely through the country scenes, that the play implies an acceptance of social change as natural, a matter of organic growth. He concludes that

> the play is about the process of social change in seventeenth-century England: the division between court and country, the mastery of nature by the arts of man, the toughness of traditional rural life in the face of political change, the hope for a regenerated England through a reunion of court with cottage, the acceptance of the processes of history.   (p. 251)

Yet Barber also finds weaknesses in the play. He calls attention to what, in his view, are its two crucial simplifications. On the one hand it leaves out 'the actual agents of change in Shakespeare's England – the engrossing merchants, the enclosing landlords, the smart lawyers, the rising yeomen'. On the other hand it solves the problems it sets in a way Barber regards as inadequate, using the supernatural 'as a substitute for plausible natural causes' (p. 252). In the end, then, Shakespeare does not quite measure up to the demands of this Marxist perspective.

There are several ways of questioning Barber's approach, though it has been little discussed by writers on the play. Rosalie Colie dismisses it in a lofty footnote as 'an interesting instance of unawareness of generic traditions' (1974, p. 249). This is to say that the play's treatment of court and country is merely conventional, not to be taken seriously as connecting with social reality. But the fact that pastoral is a form with a long-established history does not insulate it from that reality. Though the interplay of court and country is central to the convention, it does not follow that the play treats them only as literary or philosophical motifs. The Marxist critic could properly retort by pointing out Colie's failure to consider the play's political and historical context. For instance, James I notoriously heightened the division between court and country by creating many new knights – a practice humorously glanced at in the play by the Clown's joy at becoming 'a gentleman born' (V.ii.126–41). Here Barber gives only pointers. In his discussion of royal tyranny he refers to the trial and execution of Anne Boleyn (p. 239); but as I shall indicate in Section 12 there were examples nearer to hand. Later he mentions that in 1610–11 'the division between the court and the country, both politically and culturally, was becoming increasingly obvious' (pp. 243–4). This is presumably a reference to the growing conflict between King and Parliament which was to lead thirty years later to the Civil War. But the problem with Barber's case is one less of history than of interpretation. In his conclusion he commits the same error for which, earlier (p. 237), he rightly criticises D. G. James who complained that the play was a failure because it did not fit the religious myth he tailored for it. *The Winter's Tale* fails as social analysis; but perhaps that is not what it is.

A more stringent Marxist enquiry would not start from such an assumption. Barber's essay is lively and challenging, but its methods are little different from those of conventional criticism. To press such an approach further, fuller historical evidence would be needed, and also a sharper understanding of how drama relates to society.

8 Psychoanalysis

Just as there is no single Marxist approach to literature, so psychoanalysis furnishes various kinds of critical method. What has attracted psychoanalytical critics to *The Winter's Tale* is the problem of Leontes's jealousy. Critics have disputed when the jealousy begins, and whether it is motivated in any way. The psychoanalytical approach seeks not only to explain the jealousy but, at its most ambitious, to set it in a context which makes sense of the whole play.

Murray M. Schwartz begins his interpretation by summarising three earlier efforts of steadily increasing complexity (1976, pp. 203–6). First, J. I. M. Stewart proposed that Leontes reacts against a taboo love for his friend by displacing it on to Hermione and blaming her for what, unconsciously, he both wishes and fears in himself (1965, pp. 30–7). Next, C. L. Barber added an Oedipal dimension. According to Freudian theory male children have to cope with resentment stemming from the father's sexual relation to the mother. If they fail to do this, the stability of their relationships with other men in adult life is threatened. So Barber suggests that 'the primary motive which is transformed in *The Winter's Tale* . . . is the affection of Leontes for Polixenes. . . . The resolution becomes possible because the affection is consummated, as it could not otherwise be, through Perdita and Florizel'. The Freudian family romance is projected not only on to another male but another generation, with the end result of 'the daughter's loving the son as Polixenes loves the father' (1969, pp. 65, 66). Finally, Stephen Reid complicated matters further by proposing that part of the problem was Leontes's inability to accept his 'feminine self'. This leads to a parallel view of the play's resolution. If Perdita represents Leontes's feminine self and Florizel Polixenes's masculine self, then, as Schwartz puts it, the conclusion embodies 'the fulfillment of homosexual attraction in the love of Florizel and Perdita' (1976, p. 205).

Schwartz's reading is more ingenious still. In an argument too complex for convenient summary, he develops the case study in one main way. Consistently with Freudian theory, he pushes interpretation back to a still earlier stage, that of orality or the set of feelings surrounding the child's relation to the mother as its source of nourishment. This is to suggest that the relationship between Leontes and Polixenes, established so early in the play, is a myth which 'preserves in masculine form a narcissistic and idealized version of the mother's dual unity with the son' (p. 208). Also consistent with Freud is the evidence Schwartz offers, heavily dependent on unconscious puns and symbolism. For him the name Mamillius implies that 'Leontes's masculine image of himself is maternally fixated', and the choice of poison for killing Polixenes represents 'an identification with an orally catastrophic mother' (p. 220). Similarly, the sequence between Hermione and Mamillius at the start of II.i re-enacts the 'pattern of rejection and return' which Leontes cannot tolerate (p. 221). Schwartz attaches special importance to Leontes's striking image of the spider [II.i.39–45]. This, he argues, symbolises not only 'the sexually threatening mother, contact with whom signifies incest', but also 'the horror of maternal engulfment, frequently confused with the child's own oral-aggressive impulses' (p. 222). The result is that Leontes tries to 'sacrifice the catastrophic mother he tragically confuses with his child-bearing wife' (p. 224). He can be healed only by a corrective violence answering his own, in which Apollo and Paulina, standing in for father and mother, reassert their authority (p. 217).

Schwartz agrees that the play provides 'no *external* explanation of Leontes' behavior' (pp. 202–3). What he claims to have uncovered is its unconscious motivation. This in turn should connect not only with 'the potentially psychotic level of Shakespeare's psyche' (p. 219) but with 'the collective idealizing imagination of Renaissance dramatists' (p. 225). Though he does not say so, the circle is presumably completed in the unconscious of the audience. All this suggests a view of art as the acting out of fundamental human conflicts.

Strictly, it may not be possible to disprove Schwartz's reading. Nevertheless, much of it is convincing only in terms of a general theory the validity of which is far from established. It follows that, however interesting the reading may be as applied psychoanalysis, its value as criticism is limited. Too often Schwartz strains the sense in his effort to find evidence. But this is not to say that his argument is without interest for criticism. The language and action Shakespeare gives Leontes correspond very closely to what is now known as paranoid behaviour. Even more suggestive are the complementary attitudes and behaviour of the play's four main older males – Leontes, Polixenes, Antigonus and Camillo. Between these, as Schwartz says, is projected a two-sided image of woman, either sacred or devilish (pp. 209–12). Whatever the value of Freudian theory in explaining this, it is surely basic to the play.

9 Feminism

Feminist criticism is especially well equipped to handle such questions, and *The Winter's Tale* is in other ways too a promising text for feminists. It is unique among Shakespeare's plays in offering three female roles of the first importance, despite law and custom which confined all professional acting to males. At the same time its plot turns on conflicts of male attitude and behaviour towards women.

Marilyn French offers a particularly clear example of a feminist approach. She writes from the viewpoint not only of literary criticism but of feminist philosophy and politics. The context for her discussion of *The Winter's Tale* is, then, both a book on Shakespeare and a view of the whole of human culture from a feminist perspective. According to that view, history shows a division of experience in which qualities defined as 'female' are subordinated to qualities defined as 'male'. French argues that such definitions are not grounded in nature and that, consequently, division based on gender is arbitrary and subordination dangerous as well as unjust. She writes on Shakespeare not only as a major influence on Western culture but, more important, as a writer who tested the given division of experience to its limits.

For French Shakespeare's last plays are his 'final approach' to the dichotomy of 'male' and 'female' (1983, p.292). She finds that approach embodied both in form and content. First, the form is mixed. It contains qualities both 'masculine' (identified with a logical, linear plot, as in the first part of the play) and 'feminine' (identified with a freer play of associations and a greater breadth of focus, as in the pastoral scene of IV.iv). According to French the 'feminine principle' is essentially 'undramatic' because it consists in feeling, continuity and permanence. Part of Shakespeare's achievement is to give it proper theatrical expression through the form of romance, with its 'music, dance, and lyric poetry' (p. 289), but above all its existence in what French calls 'the mode of dream' (p. 286). She disputes the commonly held view that the first part of *The Winter's Tale* is 'realistic' and the second part 'mythic' (p. 308). Instead, she argues, Leontes has no rational motive for his persecution of Hermione. Neither do the irrational motives suggested by Stewart and C. L. Barber convince her. The former interpretation, she says, 'goes nowhere'; as for the latter, 'there is nothing in the text to support such a theory'. In the sense that the play's first part presents a nightmare world of male suspicion and power, it is as fully 'mythic' as the second.

French finds 'masculine' and 'feminine' qualities combined at the level of values as well as of form. For her the essential subject of the last plays 'is dual: sex and power' (p. 287). She reads all four as 'experiments in achieving a vision in which "feminine" values are triumphant within the world of earthly power' (p. 286). In *The Winter's Tale*, 'male loss of faith in the inlaw feminine principle'

(p. 338) brings about the main action, which is 'the treatment of the suspect feminine principle by a powerful male' (p. 309). By 'inlaw' she means those aspects of femininity associated with 'love, harmony, the joy of nurturance', and represented in the play by Hermione and Perdita (p. 311). Those principles Leontes takes for granted. Having tried to destroy them, to get them back he has to pay the same price paid by women for their support, in giving up his power and independence to Paulina. In this way French argues that justice is achieved by a triumph of the 'feminine'.

The value of French's approach is to demystify some of the gender assumptions dramatised by the play, and to display their consequences. She points out, for instance, that Leontes does not respond to imagined betrayal by Polixenes as he does to imagined betrayal by Hermione. As with other males in Shakespeare, 'anger at a woman . . . turns into hatred for womankind' (p. 310). She also notes the readiness which critics (usually male) have shown in forgiving Leontes, despite crimes which only fall short of murder through good fortune (p. 366). The limitation of the approach, at least as applied by French, is its abstraction. Because she discusses the play in terms of a general theory of culture, she gives little sense either of its place in history or of its qualities as theatre. Instead the concepts of 'feminine' and 'masculine' dominate. These are French's ways of summing up stock attitudes to gender which stem not from nature but conditioning, yet she allows them to take on a force of their own. Some odd judgements result. For instance, French presents Leontes and Perdita as the play's dominant figures (p. 287). Hermione and Paulina are apparently less important. For French, the former triumphs only through 'self-abasement to an extreme degree' (p. 304); while the behaviour of the latter, though 'dramatically necessary', is by implication not very admirable (p. 311). This is to ignore Hermione's passionate integrity, and Paulina's ability not only to stand up for truth and justice but help the man who inflicted wrong and suffering. It is hard not to feel that French reduces both characters because they do not easily fit her categories. The case against her approach is not that it is 'ideological'. As she says, no critical approach is free of ideology (pp. 17–18). Instead the point is that the leading ideas of her thesis are too inflexible, and that they are not sufficiently corrected against the evidence of the play.

Lisa Jardine attacks feminist studies of Shakespeare for being 'so predictable *as* criticism' (1983, p. 1). She suggests that they divide into two camps: one arguing 'that Shakespeare's genius enabled him to transcend patriarchal partisanship' (p. 2), the other that 'Shakespeare's *maleness* . . . makes it inevitable that his female characters are warped and distorted' (p. 3). She dismisses French among others severely as offering 'a timeless conflict between male and female sexuality' (p. 6). Instead she puts forward a view based not in theory but history, rejecting study of Shakespeare's characters as if they were real people for an understanding of how real people thought of 'femaleness' at the time he wrote. The result is a series of readings, not of individual texts such as *The Winter's Tale*, but of all sorts of documents which cast light on how the idea of women was constructed in the period.

This useful if astringent corrective redirects attention to history. It is not by coincidence that the most convincing feminist essay on the play combines close study of the text with an historical perspective. Patricia Southard Gourlay begins by identifying a double attitude to women in Renaissance mythography, not unlike French's separation of 'inlaw' from 'outlaw' femininity. On the one hand such figures as Venus and Eve are presented as destructively seductive, on the other hand as sources of life and creativity. Again like French, but for different reasons, Gourlay suggests that Shakespeare hit on the form of romance to explore this polarity. For the romance typically opposes a fallen world (that of 'the masculine social order') with the world of pastoral in which the feminine as ideal still reigns supreme (1975, p. 378). So far so abstract, but bringing these ideas to the play proves revealing.

First for the masculine social order. Here Gourlay argues that Leontes's behaviour is not so unaccountable as it seems. Rather, it 'makes explicit the worst assumptions of his society' (p. 378). This is borne out by the words and actions both of Polixenes and Antigonus. Gourlay points out that Shakespeare takes from his source Pandosto's attack on his daughter and transfers it to Polixenes's attack on Perdita in IV.iv. She also shows how, even when Antigonus argues with Leontes, his attitudes closely resemble his king's. Her conclusion is that 'Leontes' alienation from his wife is, in fact, symptomatic of his society's alienation from the qualities the women metaphorically represent' (p. 383). What passes for hardheaded male empiricism is cynical, reductive prejudice, a brittle barrier against male fears of sexuality.

Now for the female reversal. Between them, Gourlay suggests, Hermione, Paulina and Perdita stand for 'the subversive and creative power of love, art, and nature' (p. 378). She links Hermione and her daughter with 'the two Neoplatonic aspects of Venus, the "natural" and the "celestial"' (p. 387). Hermione offers 'grace' as 'the play's alternative to Leontes' harsh vision of reality' (p. 384); while in the pastoral scene Perdita is 'a goddess-queen, ruling in nature' (p. 387). As Gourlay points out, Paulina is a vital figure who has no precedent in any known source (p. 382). It is her role to pass through the stereotypes of scold and virago to become the architect of the play's resolution. In the process Leontes accepts as natural, lawful magic what he has previously rejected as witchcraft. Gourlay adds that these opposites match the dual idea of women which she takes to be assumed by the play.

Where Gourlay's approach might be questioned is not in its implicit feminism but in its assumptions about the relevance to *The Winter's Tale* of Renaissance occult and mythography. Hermione is not restored by magic, however miraculous the effect. Gourlay over-emphasises Paulina's powers in order to bear out her thesis. Similarly, it strains interpretation to claim that Hermione appears as a statue because she has been 'idealized into impossible perfection' (p. 390). The point, as Shakespeare's imagery of stone suggests, is the petrifying effect of Leontes's appalling denial. Until he can accept her as a whole woman she is literally dead to him. Such a reading is more consistent with a feminist perspective. The question whether it makes sense in the play's historical context cannot be answered by the intellectual history on which Gourlay depends.

The same reservation applies to a study specifically of Paulina. Carolyn Asp points out that Paulina is 'unique in English Renaissance literature' (1978, p. 145). There are no models for the role she plays as female counsellor, either in the social sphere or the political – not even in so refined a circle as that of Castiglione's *Courtier*, where women are assigned a high place. Asp proposes a figurative dimension instead: Paulina is 'the Renaissance counterpart of the female *consolatio* figure found in many medieval works' (p. 147). She then presses Boethius and Dante into service for a series of parallels from which even she cannot argue for direct influence. The argument suffers from two assumptions: that everything in Shakespeare has its source (true in a sense), and that the source is usually in high culture (certainly false, if uncongenial to much literary scholarship). Asp's contribution is in further demonstrating what a unique figure Paulina is. The nature of that uniqueness awaits definition.

10 Performance

Odd though it seems, it is only quite recently that critics have taken the evidence of theatre seriously. Some, like Charles Lamb in the early nineteenth century, have preferred Shakespeare in the theatre of the mind rather than onstage (1916). Others have turned to Shakespeare's plays for philosophy and poetry. Still others have found study of performance lacking in intellectual rigour – as compared, for instance, to study of sources and texts. There is reason for this when the emphasis is on spectacle, as in many Victorian productions. But critics can be put off too easily, and most were put off in the period when English was becoming established as a subject. Evidence from theatre is rightly distrusted when productions are plainly inadequate, though even then stage history can greatly illuminate the study of culture. But to ignore what the stage has to show is to deny the medium in which Shakespeare's drama has its being.

There are three main reasons why study of plays in performance is at least as important as any other branch of literary criticism. First, effective performance may force attention to a play which public or critics have taken for granted. Second, performers or directors may anticipate or stimulate new ways of seeing a play, whether as a whole or in details of interpretation. Third, study of performance carries a vital reminder of the human activity and social institutions without which no form of theatre could exist. Part of this is a sense of the intense, exhilarating engagement which great performances create. There is no testimony to all this more vivid than Helen Faucit's description of William Macready as Leontes, responding in the statue scene when she played Hermione for the first time:

prepared I was not, and could not be, for such a display of uncontrollable rapture. I have tried to give some idea of it;

but no words of mine could do it justice. It was the finest
burst of passionate speechless emotion I ever saw, or could
have conceived. (*Casebook*, p. 49)

As Kenneth Muir has said, it was the actors who 'taught the
critics that the statue scene could be overwhelmingly effective
in performance'. Perhaps more surprising, but equally important,
is his rider that the previous scene [V.ii] is also highly effective
when realised properly (1979, p. 171).

Dennis Bartholomeusz gives powerful evidence for all three
of the claims I have made. Discussing the New York and
London productions of 1910 and 1912, he points out a leap
in understanding important not just to the play itself but to
Shakespeare's drama generally:

the discovery of the distinctive rhythms of the swift succession
and continuity of his scenes, of the art of the direct address
of the Shakespearian actor to his audience, of the cyclical,
Elizabethan sense of time was first made in the professional
theatre through *The Winter's Tale*. (1982, p.4)

Similarly, evidence of performance enables recognition that
The Winter's Tale is 'not really a star vehicle', that the best is
brought out of it by ensemble playing, and that it is favoured
by an intimate acting area (pp. 5, 161, 79–80). Such advances in
understanding can be local as well as general, and can serve to
confirm or put in question whether a particular interpretation
is dramatically valid. The idea that Leontes is already jealous
at the start of the play has, for instance, a surprisingly long
history. Bartholomeusz shows that it goes back to Charles
Kean in the mid-nineteenth century, and the account he quotes
suggests that its theatrical expression had tact and subtlety
(p. 87). Equally interesting is the fact that certain periods rather
than others have favoured the play's realisation. Bartholomeusz
points to links in Granville-Barker's 1912 production not only
with Post-Impressionist art but, in the case of Paulina, the
Suffragette movement (pp. 140, 156). This suggests that a
successful performance depends on a kind of dialogue across
history. The London audience of 1912, or the audience wherever
whenever, responds to the Jacobean play through channels which
may differ but connect in similar social experience.

The methods of performance study are governed partly by the resources on which it depends. All kinds of theatrical records are relevant, from designs and prompt books to reviews and memoirs – and, when possible, personal experience of productions. Yet, given the importance of these resources, it would be wrong to suggest that performance study offers a uniquely privileged way of understanding Shakespeare's plays. As with any other approach, the views and assumptions of the critic must come into play and in part determine selection, emphasis and interpretation. Although Bartholomeusz presents much rich historical detail, his own reading of the play remains firmly mainstream, with its tribute to 'an organic English culture' (p. 7), and 'life inexhaustible at the roots of the earth' (p. 214). Despite his mention of Paulina as suffragette, he gives no hint of the play's political or sexual-political reach. As R. P. Draper suggests, performance study must aim 'to allow productions to tell about the dramatic possibilities inherent in the play' (1985, p. 46). But those dramatic possibilities do not exist in a vacuum, and anyone studying performance history must consider the specific historical conditions which enable or disable particular ways of presenting and responding to plays.

Part Two: Appraisal

Introduction

ANYONE sampling the critics' debate on *The Winter's Tale* soon notices that most positions have been taken up and most arguments fought on a select number of the play's most obviously dramatic sequences. Leading examples are those which show the outbreak of Leontes's jealousy in I.ii, the hunting of Antigonus and finding of Perdita in III.iii, the sheep-shearing feast in IV.iv, and the whole of the statue scene [V.iii]. I will not concentrate discussion on any of these except for the last, but instead approach the play by considering several related topics. Though they are topics I believe to be central, I do not offer them as keys for breaking a code, as in some allegorical and thematic interpretation. Shakespeare's drama is never schematic and resists all attempts to reduce it. Instead I will put forward some alternative ways of understanding the play. This will include setting in a different light sequences which critics have favoured, and pointing up others which they have tended to neglect. As should be clear from Part One, two main convictions guide my approach. First, I believe that the play is essentially of the theatre and that no understanding which fails to respond to its theatricality can be adequate. Second, I believe that the play raises social and political questions which are as important as those questions of religion, morality and philosophy which most previous critics have addressed. In short, I think that in trying to make sense of the play it is a mistake to abstract it either from the medium of performance or from the processes of history.

11 Entertainment

The opening scenes especially of Shakespeare's mature plays repay the closest attention. Like *King Lear*, *The Winter's Tale* begins by introducing the central dramatic action obliquely, through the comments of subordinate figures – one of whom, Archidamus, appears only in this scene. The play begins easily and naturally, as two courtiers enter in conversation. Like others by Shakespeare it illustrates the principle reversed by Tom Stoppard, in *Rosencrantz and Guildenstern are Dead*, of 'every exit being an entrance somewhere else' (1967, p. 21). The dramatic sequence is so fully imagined that, when characters enter, they invariably carry with them a sense of the place they have left. Archidamus and Camillo are talking about 'entertainment' [I.i.8]. As John Lucas suggests, in a brilliant uncollected essay from which I have learned much, the tone and character of what they say indicate that they have just left a banquet (1982, p. 6).

The reason for this lavish entertainment is to celebrate friendship – between Leontes and Polixenes, between subjects such as themselves. Towards the end of the scene Camillo provides a vivid image of friendship when he says that Leontes and Polixenes have 'shook hands as over a vast; and embraced, as it were, from the ends of opposed winds' [29–31]. As the Victorian critic W. E. Henley pointed out, this evokes a well-known visual representation of amity in the emblem books of the period (Furness, 1964, p. 8). So the image is not only arresting in itself. It symbolises the mutual affection between persons and nations which is about to be broken. And John Lucas has shown how it becomes a vital motif of the play (1982, pp. 5–9).

If Camillo and Archidamus paint an idyllic picture of mutual friendship, it is strange that the same emblems torment Leontes when, a few minutes' playing time later, he erupts into jealousy. His phrase 'To mingle friendship far' [I.ii.109] suggests that Hermione and Polixenes have joined hands. Editors usually take the hint with a stage direction to that effect, as Schanzer does in the Penguin text. Leontes goes on to pervert the idea of 'entertainment' [111], repeating the word at the end of his speech: 'O, that is entertainment/ My bosom likes not, nor my brows!' [118–19]. Later he will corrupt it utterly by asking Camillo to poison Polixenes, while he (in Camillo's words) maintains 'a countenance as clear/ As friendship wears at feasts' [I.ii.343–4]. What had been an emblem of amity becomes a proof of betrayal, and then a threat of death.

Interpretations of *The Winter's Tale* often divide on the question of Leontes's jealousy: whether it is motivated or not, or, if it is taken to be motivated, what the essential motive is. Those who read the play either from a religious or from a specifically Christian standpoint, like Wilson Knight or S. L. Bethell, usually assign no motive. They see Leontes's plunge into jealousy as both symptom and effect of the fall of man. Conversely psychoanalytical critics, like Murray Schwartz, detect motives for jealousy of almost endless complexity in the unconscious they find in the play. I do not wish to deny the plausibility of either type of reading, only their claim to provide total, inclusive explanations. For what the language and action suggest is that Leontes's jealousy is precipitated by the very fullness of Hermione's hospitality.

The role Hermione has to play in the scene is that of 'kind hostess' [60]. Later, during her trial, she describes her behaviour to Polixenes in terms which there is no reason whatever to doubt:

> I do confess
> I loved him as in honour he required:
> With such a kind of love as might become
> A lady like me; with a love even such,
> So and no other, as yourself commanded;
> Which not to have done I think had been in me
> Both disobedience and ingratitude
> To you and toward your friend.
>
> [III.ii.61–8]

This account corresponds to the stage action, in which Hermione takes on the task of persuading Polixenes to stay at her husband's command, 'Tongue-tied, our queen? Speak you' [I.ii.27], and succeeds only too well in it. But what it does not and cannot suggest is the stage effect, both visual and aural. The following scene, in Shakespeare's continuous action, shows that Hermione is heavily pregnant. Along with the sense of fertility her pregnant body conveys is her rich, sensual and even innocently suggestive language:

> Cram's with praise, and make's
> As fat as tame things . . . .
> Our praises are our wages. You may ride's
> With one soft kiss a thousand furlongs ere
> With spur we heat an acre.
>
> [91–6]

Hermione speaks here of a need for praise presented as typically feminine. It is capable, however, of being mistaken for openness to seduction. Her langorous elisions ('Cram's', 'make's', 'ride's') not only add to the heady sound effects of the lines, partly through sibilance, but suggest a tempting receptiveness. The underlying metaphors are sinister – an animal being fattened for slaughter (a word she uses in the same lines [93]), a horse being ridden voluntarily to the limits of its endurance. They also have sexual implications, especially 'ride' and perhaps 'heat' two lines later. Few members of an audience might register such meanings consciously, but the associative nature of the verse allows for cumulative, subliminal effects.

Without at present exploring further the onset of Leontes's jealousy, I wish to link this scene of lavish entertainment with another later in the play. The structural parallels between its two parts have often been pointed out, for example in Ernest Schanzer's work discussed in Part One. But among these the theme of entertainment has received little notice. The sheep-shearing scene opens with a dialogue between Florizel and Perdita, but does not get under way until the guests enter. Florizel then tells Perdita: 'Address yourself to entertain them sprightly' [IV.iv.53], and the Shepherd seconds him by painting a colourful picture of his wife as hostess. Despite her modesty Perdita does not fail him. At his request she shows true hospitality by welcoming first those guests who are not only uninvited but unknown. This is a country equivalent to the scene from which Archidamus and Camillo entered at the play's beginning. Not only does it not suffer in comparison, but it unfolds in relaxed, carefree celebration until Polixenes, like Leontes before him, explodes. But his outburst, unlike his brother king's, is very plainly motivated. Perdita's grace as a hostess may recall Hermione's, but it is Florizel's defiance of his father which provokes fury. This suggests the influence of other factors again.

12 Power, place, patriarchy

Though hardly on the same scale as Leontes's outburst earlier in the play, Polixenes's anger breaks up the feast and is a violent, ungrateful return for the Shepherd's hospitality. His threats of vindictive punishment echo his brother king's, but there is reversal as well as repetition. Camillo, the same wise counsellor who helped him escape Leontes's anger, now takes the part of his own threatened victims. One question this ironic parallel raises is what enables, and apparently authorises, such arbitrary, disrupting behaviour.

An obvious fact often taken for granted in discussion of *The Winter's Tale* is that its two most dangerous characters are kings. It is easy to ignore this as mere convention or dramatic convenience, but there is ample evidence that the play takes absolute power and its abuse seriously. Part of this is the repeated outrage of broken entertainment, especially through its impact on the stage. But much of it consists in Leontes's presentation in the first part of the play.

The full, resonant effect of Hermione's speeches in I.ii could hardly contrast more strongly than with her husband's sour, peremptory rhythms during the same sequence. His speeches are all clipped, even curt, and his main voice is the imperative:

> Stay your thanks a while,
> And pay them when you part.
> [9–10]

> We are tougher, brother,
> Than you can put us to't.
> [15–16]

> One sev'n-night longer.
> [17]

> We'll part the time between's then; and in that
> I'll no gainsaying.
> [18-19]

> Tongue-tied, our queen? Speak you.
> [27]

These speeches are sometimes cited as evidence that Leontes is already jealous as the scene begins. That is, at least, a possibility in the theatre, though for sheer dramatic effect a contrast between apparent well-being and sudden, overwhelming passion is certainly stronger. But Leontes's curtness is also in keeping with possession of unchecked power enjoyed from an early age. The twenty-three years he refers to as separating him from childhood [I.ii.155] mark him as less than thirty. F. W. Bateson has pointed out that, according to the traditional scheme of the four ages of man, this places him early within the choleric period (1978, pp. 72-3). But it is also a young age at which to hold absolute power, with no moderating influence stronger than that of Camillo who is indebted to him for patronage [I.ii.313–14]. No wonder if Leontes is volatile and unstable. No wonder if he will brook neither denial when he asks Polixenes to stay nor, when his persuasions fail, the success of Hermione's. 'At my request he would not', is his immediate response [I.ii.87]. Like Polixenes later, the king expects to be obeyed.

The dangers of absolute power are thrown into relief by the king's madness. Possessed by jealousy, Leontes has in effect the power to define reality according to his fantasy. He casts Hermione in prison as if she were guilty, and commits her child to the jeopardy of nature. Through a show trial he seeks to impose belief on his subjects, who can resist only at personal hazard. Camillo demonstrates one way of responding. He simply cannot believe Leontes's charge against Hermione, and his outspoken denial, 'You never spoke what did become you less/Than this' [I.ii.282–3], is a dangerous risk. When Leontes insists even more violently, only one reply will keep Camillo safe: 'I must believe you, sir' [333]. Here 'must' can mean compulsion as well as conviction. This is the first of four equivocations in which Camillo takes refuge; the others, in 'fetch off' [334], 'removed' [335] and 'Account me not your servant' [347] are pointed out by Schanzer (1969, p. 171). They are his response to Leontes's order to poison Polixenes, which sets an impossible dilemma. To disobey is not only to jeopardise himself and his position, but to break his oath of allegiance. To obey is not only to commit murderous injustice, but to break the taboo against striking 'anointed kings' [358]. Camillo is in the wrong whatever he does, thanks to the power of monarchy. He chooses the lesser evil, with all the costs it entails. Shakespeare spends over half of a long scene on the dialogues between Leontes and Camillo, then Camillo and Polixenes. The sequence is sometimes criticised for its length, and modern directors often make cuts in it. Jacobean audiences, closer to the political realities it demonstrates, probably found it more compelling.

As a weak man, essentially a bully, Leontes illustrates what might be called the pathology of monarchy. Part of this is his volatile, ungovernable behaviour; part his swiftness to pull rank when apparently threatened. In the first two scenes in which he appears Leontes rarely uses the royal 'we' to which his rank entitles him. When, however, his courtiers question his actions, he is quick to reassert it:

> Why, what need we
> Commune with you of this, but rather follow
> Our forceful instigation? Our prerogative
> Calls not your counsels, but our natural goodness
> Imparts this . . . .
>
> . . . . The matter,
> The loss, the gain, the ord'ring on't, is all
> Properly ours
>
> [II.i.161–70]

Similarly he resumes the royal 'we' in commanding Antigonus to expose Perdita [II.iii.169–78], and exploits it while he still retains control in the trial scene. The stilted language is equally characteristic ('Commune', 'instigation', 'prerogative', 'Imparts'). As Jonathan Smith has observed in an illuminating article, two kinds of language struggle in Leontes: 'the Latinate diction which, as he sees it, befits a king', and 'an Othello-like language, coarse and full-blooded, which means chaos' (1968, p. 318). Smith establishes how unusual is much of the king's vocabulary. Leontes's language in the play's first part is not only that of a man possessed. It is also that of a king desperately seeking to assert his authority.

Polixenes echoes Leontes's use of the royal 'we' when he breaks up the sheep-shearing feast. He uses it even when addressing his son, though he does not sustain it for the whole speech: 'we'll bar thee from succession; / Not hold thee of our blood, no, not our kin' [IV.iv.426–7]. To complete the parallel, Leontes in his madness shows the same insistence on distinctions of rank as Polixenes does in his rage at Florizel's courtship of Perdita. Questioning Camillo about Hermione's conduct with Polixenes, he expresses contempt for 'the common blocks' and 'Lower messes' [I.ii.225, 227]. As the eighteenth-century editor George Steevens put it, 'Leontes comprehends inferiority of understanding in the idea of inferiority of rank' (Furness, 1964, p. 42). Again, accusing Hermione, Leontes refuses her the privilege of rank 'Lest barbarism . . . Should a like language use to all degrees, / And mannerly distinguishment leave out / Betwixt the prince and beggar' [II.i.84–7]. It is only when he has been cured of his jealousy, and served his penitence, that he can plead for the suspending of just such a distinction. Crucially, it is before Perdita's birth is known that he agrees to persuade Polixenes to permit the marriage of a prince and, if not quite a beggar, a shepherdess [V.i.228–32].

If monarchy and hierarchy are two of the principles which support Leontes in his injustice, a third and no less important is patriarchy. One reason why a man, and especially a king, is so jealous of his wife is fear of disabling his succession. The woman is treated as property – 'his pond' or his 'gates', in Leontes's demeaning imagery [I.ii.195–7] – and she can hardly be trusted away from him. By extension, a woman who resists male power is stigmatised as a witch. Polixenes, accusing Perdita of seducing his son, calls her 'fresh piece / Of excellent witchcraft' [IV.iv.419–20], and Leontes calls the defiant Paulina 'A mankind witch!' [II.iii.67]. It is the three principles of monarchy, hierarchy and patriarchy which prevent the courtiers from intervening effectively with Leontes once Camillo has escaped with Polixenes. Not only are they too deferential, too easily intimidated. The fact that they share the same principles restrains them. Antigonus, the most outspoken, shows the closeness of his assumptions to his king's in vowing to geld his daughters if Hermione is guilty, so that they cannot 'bring false generations' [II.i.148]. Conversely Dion and Cleomenes later try to persuade Leontes to remarry to prevent 'fail of issue' [V.i.27]. Antigonus compromises far enough to agree to expose Perdita, and jumps to the conclusion that Hermione is guilty on the dubious evidence of his dream [III.iii.38–45]. It is telling that only Paulina, who has no other power than strength of personality, is able to stand up to Leontes convincingly. For her pains her husband is taunted with weakness in not being able to control his supposed inferior.

The question of the play's relation to ideology is complex. On the one hand Paulina may appear an early feminist; on the other Shakespeare has her expect that Hermione's child will be a boy [II.ii.26]. He then performs a further reversal, for it is the daughter who ensures the succession. To give another example, Leontes says in welcoming Florizel: 'Your mother was most true to wedlock, Prince: / For she did print your royal father off,

/ Conceiving you' [V.i.123–5]. His metaphor diminishes the woman's reproductive role to the passivity of paper. Yet, however characteristic the attitude in its period, it would be rash to assume it is Shakespeare's. Not only is it consistent with Leontes's earlier behaviour – his obsession with legitimacy still shows – but the play has already demonstrated the dangers of such attitudes.

There is historical evidence to back the claim that the play raises questions concerning royal power, rank and male dominance. Simon Shepherd, for instance, calls attention to a highly topical scandal which draws together a number of threads both in contemporary politics and the play. In March 1610 King James forbade his cousin Arbella Stuart to marry William Seymour. When they defied him he first had the man imprisoned in the Tower, from which he escaped in July 1611, and then – for life – the woman. Shepherd comments:

> The plays of this date contain references to imprisoned lovers, secret marriages, foreign escapes. The story was interesting because it highlighted James's harshness and arbitrariness. The monarch in charge of a corrupt court oppresses two young lovers. Anything that laid bare James's authoritarian attitudes must have struck home in 1610 because of the debate between king and Parliament over royal prerogative.
>
> (1981, p. 119)

John Lucas adds:

> Leontes's mad claim that 'There is a plot against my life, my crown' [II.i.47] echoes James's paranoid fears that he was surrounded by assassins, just as his method of disposing of those he distrusted may well be reflected in Leontes's plan to have Camillo poison Polixenes's drink.   (1982, p. 3).

One the other hand, *The Winter's Tale* is known to have been enjoyed by James when it was presented at court, and it was considered a safe enough choice of play to be staged for him on the anniversary of the Gunpowder Plot (Pafford, 1963, p. 25). Either it does not raise political questions, or James cannot have recognised questions which might bear critically on him. The way beyond this impasse lies in recognising the special character of the play's theatre.

13 Theatricality

In obvious ways *The Winter's Tale* is a highly theatrical play. Leontes's jealousy fills the first half with dramatic tension. It is complemented in the second half by the sheep-shearing scene which runs the gamut of entertainment from dance and song to graceful romance and broad comedy. Each part ends with a dramatic coup: the sudden entrance of a bear to pursue Antigonus offstage, the apparent coming to life of a statue. In between there is the frankly theatrical device of Father Time, conjuring acceptance of the play's illusions.

But *The Winter's Tale* exploits the resources of theatre in more complex ways than any such list can suggest. Shakespeare wrote his plays for performance in various acting areas, including the Globe and Blackfriars stages but also platforms improvised at court or on tour. They require no scenery and few properties, though costumes were probably varied and rich. The last plays are often likened to the masques which enjoyed so much success at the period. But they depend far less on sheer visual spectacle than the comparison suggests, and none requires any extraordinary theatrical effects. It follows that they had to meet two main demands. They required actors of great ability, not only in speech and gesture but often also in dance and music. And they required outstanding art from the playwright in creating dramatic conditions which would draw in and hold an audience very largely through the mere use of words. The theatricality of *The Winter's Tale* includes much disarming entertainment, though without factitious illusion. Even more, however, it consists in inviting or compelling moral participation and response.

Such an aim is clear both from Shakespeare's changes to his source and from his choices of dramatic focus. As Ernest Schanzer points out, Shakespeare reduces the role played by Fortune and emphasises 'human purpose': 'It is man's wishes, fears, and imaginings, rather than Fortune, Providence, or the gods, which are depicted as the prime movers of the play's events' (1969, pp. 39–40). Correspondingly Shakespeare chose not to present the Delphic oracle onstage, though this did little to deter Victorian merchants in spectacle. Instead there is the brief scene [III.i] of Cleomenes and Dion returning. Their twenty-two lines of quiet, reverent conversation suggest how dramatic poetry may outweigh any amount of scenery.

The words of Cleomenes and Dion work by bringing imagination into play. If the words succeed, the audience are not
merely spectators. They are involved in an active process of
exchange. The most theatrical scenes are those which deny
even more strongly the relation of a mere spectator. Soon after
his first outburst of jealousy Leontes launches into a shocking
speech which turns from his son to the audience:

> Go play, boy, play: thy mother plays, and I
> Play too – but so disgraced a part, whose issue
> Will hiss me to my grave. Contempt and clamour
> Will be my knell. Go play, boy, play. There have been,
> Or I am much deceived, cuckolds ere now;
> And many a man there is, even at this present,
> Now, while I speak this, holds his wife by th'arm,
> That little thinks she has been sluiced in's absence,
> And his pond fished by his next neighbour, by
> Sir Smile, his neighbour.
>
> [I.ii.187–96]

Part of the effect of this speech is to renew awareness of
the dramatic medium and then to turn that awareness back on
the audience. The metaphors from theatre ('play', 'part', 'issue',
'hiss') call attention to the fact that Leontes is only an actor. Then,
the dramatic illusion broken, the males in the audience are put
on the spot about their own sexual fears and suspicions. It is a
humorous but also an uncomfortable moment. Shakespeare uses
the flexibility of an open acting space to connect audience to play-
er. Leontes's jealousy is likely to appear both more plausible and
more disturbing for those who have been jolted into recognising
its likeness to their own secret suspicions.

Another way in which Shakespeare involves and perhaps
disturbs the audience is to encourage responses which contradict
each other. In II.iii Paulina brings the baby Perdita to Leontes
in an attempt to heal his mad jealousy. He reacts with the
frightening arbitrariness of a tyrant, threatening Hermione,
Perdita and Paulina with burning, and ending with the order
of exposing Perdita to what seems certain death. On the other
hand, as Paulina stoutly resists and counter-attacks, the scene
sets up unmistakable opportunities for laughter. These begin with
Paulina's entry, as Leontes says to Antigonus: 'I charged thee that

she should not come about me. / I knew she would' [II.iii.43–4].
It is the rueful 'I knew she would' that is impossible to take
straight, pointing as it does to Leontes's knowledge of Paulina's
forcefulness and his own weakness in face of it. Next, though easy
to neglect in reading the play, the effect of the baby on stage is
important. It pulls two ways, showing Leontes's inhumanity but
also enabling comic embarrassment. Some productions take the
cue by having Paulina place the baby in his arms. Whether the
action is pushed as far as this or not, the scene presents further
comic collisions. Paulina insists, repeating the word six times
(and three times in a single line), that Hermione is Leontes's
'good queen' [58–65]. Then she bluntly returns his charge of
henpecking by wishing only that he feared his wife too [80–1].
When Leontes tries to reassert himself by threatening death
from burning, she responds not only by pressing on with her
argument but by humorously insulting him: 'It [i.e. the child]
is yours; / And, might we lay th'old proverb to your charge,
/ So like you, 'tis the worse' [95–7]. The speech ends with a
comparison that is utterly absurd – so absurd that editors have
been debating ever since whether she (or Shakespeare) could have
meant it. Paulina asks that Nature give the baby Perdita no touch
of jealousy, 'lest she suspect, as he does, / Her children not her
husband's' [106–7]. It is possible to explain this by saying that
Paulina falls into absurdity unintentionally in her rush of excited
speech. But it is equally possible that Shakespeare has her mean it
deliberately, to show up the ridiculousness of Leontes's suspicion.
Either way it is a notably comic moment among several in a scene
that had every chance to be solemn. And Paulina's exit strikes
just the same note as her entrance when she mockingly insists
on going in her own time, without compulsion: 'So, so. Farewell,
we are gone' [129].

In the exchanges between Paulina and Leontes Shakespeare in
one sense exploits the stereotype of the scold or virago. Paulina
affronts patriarchy by taking on not only her husband but her
king, and much of the humour in the scene grows out of this
irreverent reversal. In another sense, however, Shakespeare also
disables the stereotype, or at least makes it difficult to uphold
comfortably, creating again a dilemma for the audience. For it
is Leontes the tyrant and madman who appeals to the stereotype
most, accusing Antigonus for allowing himself to be henpecked,
charging that Paulina is 'A mankind witch' [67]. Women, it should

be remembered, were burned in Shakespeare's day and later for the crimes which Leontes alleges; and King James wrote a book on witchcraft. But the play turns such charges round. Not only does Paulina cast herself in the role she will later play, as Leontes's 'physician' and 'most obedient counsellor' [54-5]. She also has one of the best lines in the scene, and the play, when she rejects Leontes's threat with the words: 'It is an heretic that makes the fire, / Not she which burns in't' [114-15]. The result of all this is a scene whose theatricality consists in the contradictory responses it calls for: concern and laughter; amusement at the reversal of roles and respect for Paulina's brave, no-nonsense integrity; most of all, complicity with the stereotype of the man-taming woman and discomfort when the action exposes its inadequacy. Again, it is a sequence that asks questions, presses examination of stock beliefs and responses.

Shakespeare uses the same theatrical method in scenes which raise human or existential rather than political or ideological questions. The best example is III.iii, in which Antigonus and the mariners are lost and Perdita found. On the one hand what happens is horrifying. A ship is being wrecked with all hands, an old man is being hunted by a bear which will eat him, and a baby lies exposed to the elements as well as to wild beasts. The bear bursting onstage was probably played by an actor. Scholarship has turned up no certain records of live bears appearing in the theatre, and the practical difficulties would have been difficult if not impossible to surmount (see Biggins, 1962). But there is no reason why a simulated bear, appearing unexpectedly and briefly, should not be capable of creating shock and fear. If this is so, the action goes on to change key in a way which seems completely inappropriate. No sooner has Antigonus fled the stage than he is replaced by the Shepherd comically ruminating as he finds Perdita: 'They were warmer that got this than the poor thing is here' [III.iii.73-4]. Then the Clown follows with his unintentionally hilarious description of the two appalling sights he has just seen, so excited that he cannot keep them separate. What is startling about this is that the Clown's down-to-earth language conveys almost brutally the physical horror of what he is reporting:

O, the most piteous cry of the poor souls! Sometimes to
see 'em, and not to see 'em: now the ship boring the moon

with her mainmast, and anon swallowed with yeast and froth,
as you'd thrust a cork into a hogshead. And then for the
land-service: to see how the bear tore out his shoulder bone,
how he cried to me for help, and said his name was Antigonus,
a nobleman.   [88-94]

For all the out-of-place language, and the Clown's attempt
to tell two strange sights at once, this is not simply comic
distancing. The scene does not mark a transition from tragedy
to comedy, as has often been suggested. Rather the audience is
being asked to attend at one and the same time to mortal suffering
and humorous incongruity. Again the sequence is contradictory,
simultaneously tragic and comic. It seems designed to convey the
shocking co-existence of living and dying, suffering and renewal.
It is hardly an accidental symmetry which has an old man
stumbling on birth and a young man on death.

Such questions are open to the audience to take up or
ignore, like the political and ideological questions which, I
have argued, certain sequences set. But if part of the play's
dramatic potential consists in disturbing and questioning the
audience, another part consists in disarming it. Leontes may be
understood as a study in irresponsible male power. To James, a
propagandist for monarchy who thought well of himself as king,
a different response was available. How could so unimpressive a
figure as Leontes evoke his own place and authority? How could
a romance, with its marvels and spectacles, bear on the real world
around him?

Other parts of the play work hard at achieving this kind of
disarming. Not only does Shakespeare surround his presentation
of madness, violence and death with playful artificiality. He also
plays conscious games with his audience's awareness. No contemporary could have failed to recognise the deliberate paradox in his
transposition of Sicilia and Bohemia. This is a witty departure
not only from his source, Greene's *Pandosto*, which was very well
known, but from familiar pastoral convention. With the same
irreverence Bohemia gets its seacoast and, in keeping with Time's
speech in IV.i, anachronisms flourish. The same kind of playful
inversion and parody also figure in the dialogue and action. Again
and again Shakespeare contrives not only to have things both ways
but even to use the audience's awareness to enable this. I will try
to illustrate each of these theatrical gambits.

S.L. Bethell pointed out the multiple layers of illusion in Perdita's role at the sheep-shearing feast: 'boy acting girl who is a princess supposed to be a shepherdess acting as make-believe princess' (*Casebook*, p. 125). Shakespeare brings two of these layers together to produce dramatic irony. Camillo calls Perdita 'The queen of curds and cream' [IV.iv.161]. But Florizel has already told her, in an unconscious pun, that she so 'Crowns' what she does that all her acts 'are queens' [145–6]; and Polixenes has observed that 'nothing she does or seems / But smacks of something greater than herself, / Too noble for this place' [157–9]. Shakespeare presents Perdita as princess by nature as well as by birth. The sheer transparency of the ploy, not just its dramatic realisation, makes it easier to accept. There is the same playful contrivance in Perdita's argument with Polixenes over the ethics of grafting. Both are contradicted yet in the end proved right by the dramatic situation. Shakespeare seeks to naturalise his art by a kind of theatrical framing.

A similar self-reference is part of the drama's verbal display. Not content with switching Sicilia with Bohemia, Shakespeare introduces pastoral metaphors into courtly scenes, and courtly concerns into pastoral. To give only a few examples, the opening scene has a courtier talk horticulture; 'They were trained together in their childhoods; and there rooted betwixt them such an affection, which cannot choose but branch now' [I.i.22–4]. Polixenes picks up the pastoral language a few moments later in his first speech: 'Nine changes of the watery star hath been / The shepherd's note since we have left our throne / Without a burden' [I.ii.1–3]. Conversely Autolycus makes his first entry like a breath of fresh air, singing of spring in the country. Yet he interrupts his song to mention serving in court, and later plays the courtier over the Shepherd and his son. These verbal sleights of hand are especially clear in the play Shakespeare makes with his title. A winter's tale was an idle story, of the sort Mamillius begins to tell his mother ('A sad tale's best for winter' [II.i.25]) when Leontes enters in fury. As has often been suggested, this entrance identifies Leontes with the man who, in the story, 'Dwelt by a churchyard' [30]. The gambit is to juxtapose with an acknowledged fiction, a mere tale, a dramatic fiction which, by its startling intrusion, carries all the appearance of reality. Shakespeare exploits this repeatedly in the second-to-last scene. Here, by insisting so much on how incredible the story is, the courtiers invite its acceptance. If the audience is aware that the play is almost as unlikely a story as one of Autolycus's ballads, Shakespeare trumps that awareness by having the play admit it: 'Such a deal of wonder is broken out within this hour that ballad-makers cannot be able to express it . . . . This news, which is called true, is so like an old tale that the verity of it is in strong suspicion' [V.ii.23–9]. The beauty of the device is that its success does not depend on literal belief. It encourages indulgence by drawing humorous attention to its own artificiality. Part of the humour stems from the wonderful dramatic propriety by which this affected, sophisticated talk is given to courtiers; just as, earlier, the telling of a winter's tale was perfectly apt to Mamillius's relationship with Hermione.

The play's disarming effect is in keeping with the 'note of tolerant understanding' which Granville-Barker identified as its keynote (1974, p. 19). Yet, though the play certainly allows such an effect, it does not represent all its potential. As has also been pointed out, Shakespeare used the definite article in his title: not 'a winter's tale', suggesting a mere romance, but 'The Winter's Tale', the essential story of winter itself. Whatever resonances of seasonal myths this may imply, the play is firmly centred in human interaction. To convey the nature of winter in human relationships more is required even than tolerance and understanding. I will try to show this by discussing the role of Autolycus.

14 Autolycus

If the stage direction 'Exit, pursued by a bear' [III.iii.57] may be taken to end the first part of *The Winter's Tale*, 'Enter Autolycus, singing' may be taken to begin the second [IV.iii.0; repeated at IV.iv.219]. The play is sparse in such instructions but these two help make up by their laconic directness. Yet the apparent contrast between bizarre horror and carefree entertainment is not as neat as it seems. Just as the Clown's description makes Antigonus's death grotesquely comic as well as horrifying, so Autolycus is not simply a source of melodious humour.

There are two ways of sentimentalising the role. The first is to present Autolycus as a lovable rogue, a kind of mellowed Falstaff. So, with unconscious innuendo, Edward Dowden fancied that

Shakespeare 'conceived his Autolycus . . . in some Warwickshire field, one breezy morning, as the daffodil began to peer' (*Casebook*, p. 37). The second is a theatrical counterpart to this literary whimsy: the part is played to the full for all the comic opportunities it will yield. So, in his survey of the role on the stage, John Russell Brown declares: 'In the theatre Autolycus must be a clown's star performance, or nothing' (1966, p. 103). His main illustration is the vivid humour of William Burton, the great nineteenth-century American clown. It is this view of Autolycus which still dominates productions. R.P. Draper describes four recent examples of extravagant comic invention (1985, pp. 66–9), to which at the time of writing Joe Melia is adding further (Royal Shakespeare Company, 1986–7). The reasons for such an emphasis are obvious: Autolycus is a fund of dramatic vitality and easily accessible gags. The danger is in giving him a kind and a degree of prominence which the text is at pains to qualify.

Autolycus certainly has his importance. His role is the third longest in the play, after those of Leontes and Paulina. He sings five of the play's six songs, taking a leading role in the other, and accompanies not only two of his entrances with songs but two of his exits [IV.iii.121–4; IV.iv.313–21]. These go far towards establishing the holiday atmosphere of the sheep-shearing scene, quite apart from his contribution to its comic side through tricks and repartee. For such reasons Wilson Knight calls Autolycus 'a figure of absolute comedy', 'spring incarnate' (*Casebook*, pp. 136, 137). But Knight also catches an ambivalence in Autolycus which needs emphasising. He is apparently the first to have noticed that the sequence in which Autolycus robs the Clown is 'a clear parody of the parable of the Good Samaritan' (p. 138). Later he goes on to point out an extra twist to the comparison with Falstaff. As each man's exploitation of his victims is further exposed to the audience, his attractions begin to tarnish and by the end each has been effectively faded out. For Knight it is as essential that Autolycus lose his 'dramatic dignity' as it is for Falstaff to be rejected. Otherwise the play's '"high seriousness"' is compromised (p. 150).

Knight argues that for the sake of larger significances Shakespeare has Autolycus and Falstaff undergo moral-dramatic declines. Though I cannot pursue the comparison, there is evidence of a double edge to both roles from the outset. In the first words of his opening song Autolycus couples daffodils with doxies (i.e. prostitutes). He goes on to relish the sight of a sheet inviting theft with as much gusto as the sound of birdsong, and he ends his impromptu ballad by pointing to his occupational hazard of the stocks. The robbing of the Clown is also less conventionally comic than it looks. First, the Clown's naïveté contains pathos as well as humour: 'Alack, poor soul! Thou hast need of more rags to lay on thee, rather than have these off . . . . Alas, poor man! A million of beating may come to a great matter' [IV.iii.53–9]. Second, once Autolycus has shown his superior wit and dexterity by picking the Clown's pocket, the joke is turned against him. For the Clown's compassion has him try to give Autolycus some of the money he has just stolen, provoking a comically anxious cover-up. In a double irony, the Clown's offer outdoes Autolycus's satirical comment, 'You ha'done me a charitable office' [75]. He will later renew the thief's anxiety by offering to help him home. Similarly, the Clown bluntly punctures Autolycus's elaborate in-joke about the identity of his supposed attacker: 'Not a more cowardly rogue in all Bohemia. If you had but looked big and spit at him, he'd have run'[102–3].

The fact that the play offers ample comic opportunity to the Clown as well as to Autolycus was not lost on eighteenth-century actors, and Dennis Bartholomeusz cites several famous examples (1982, pp. 34–5). But this too is easy to exaggerate. The two roles have a different kind of ambivalence. Autolycus invites recognition of what a thoroughly amoral energy would mean, the Clown of the moral benefits of simplicity. It is as if the play were anticipating Swift's dilemma, in *A Tale of a Tub*, between fool and knave. Once more its dramatic potential is at its sharpest in setting questions of response.

Nevertheless, the play gives only light emphasis to Autolycus's thieving at the feast. Autolycus responds to the offered entertainment no more gratefully than Polixenes, but none of his victims is shown regretting or even noticing losses. Instead his own success is turned against him. Shakespeare exploits a stock comic situation in having him crow so triumphantly to himself that he fails, till too late, to realise how close he is to giving himself away to Camillo, Florizel and Perdita who are still onstage: 'If they have overheard me now – why, hanging' [IV.iv.622–3]. Insult joins potential injury with Camillo's suggestion that they 'make an instrument of this, omit / Nothing may give us aid' [620–1]. So much for Autolycus's complacency; he comically repeats 'I am a poor fellow, sir' [626, 634]. But none of this chastens him. Alone again onstage he continues to brag, renewing his offer to the audience of colluding in his candid villainy. Once more, though, there is a twist to this. 'I see this is the time that the unjust man doth thrive' [669–70] has a Biblical ring, telling against him (see Pafford, 1963, p. 127); and the phrase 'his clog at his heels' [674–5] for Perdita and Florizel shows a limited, even sordid cynicism.

   It is the sequence that follows with the Shepherd and Clown which demonstrates most. Autolycus pulls rank over his two supposed inferiors by posing as a courtier. They show simplicity in being so easily deceived; though the fact that they fail to recognise either Autolycus or the clothing he has got from Florizel is thanks to convention. But their perplexity and deference are convincing. If Autolycus is what he claims to be, there is every reason to propitiate him – as Autolycus has just propitiated Camillo. Similarly, the Clown's confusion of two kinds of court is unconsciously satirical. He knows that both courtier and judge may need bribing, so his 'Advocate's the court-word for a pheasant' [IV.iv.737] is not simply a humorous error. Autolycus's threats bring the sequence to its climax. On the one hand his relentless exaggeration is comic, especially as he dwells on every detail of the torture he describes for the Clown. There is humour also in the Clown's all too anxious concern: 'Has the old man e'er a son, sir, do you hear, an't like you, sir?' [777–8]. On the other hand the relish Autolycus shows is unpleasant, and it is highlighted by three dramatic parallels. Most immediately his threats recall those of Polixenes earlier in the same scene, but they also look back, at a further remove, to those of Leontes before him. It is not only that, as J. H. P. Pafford has said, there is 'a faint rhythmic parallel to the evil in Leontes' (1963, p. lxxx). The nature of the parallel, abuse of power, connects them more closely. This thematic tie is clinched by an image echoing the most spectacular moment so far in the play: 'though authority be a stubborn bear, yet he is oft led by the nose with gold' [796–7]. Autolycus, whose name means 'wolf's self', is momentarily linked with the play's three images of disruptive power.

   Paradoxically, it is through his encounter with the Shepherd and Clown that Autolycus makes his sole contribution to the plot. This is in diverting the two from Polixenes to his former master Florizel, whom he has already provided with a disguise.

But he can claim little credit for his assistance. The exchange of clothes is commanded, the meeting accidental, and the diversion self-confessed 'knavery' [IV.iv.677]. When he finds out the Clown and Shepherd's purpose, his motive turns to sheer self-interest. The scene ends with a clear hint that he will bring about the expected comic discovery, in which Perdita's identity will be revealed. That the expectation is disappointed has puzzled some. For instance, in his complaints about Shakespeare's workmanship in *The Winter's Tale*, Sir Arthur Quiller-Couch claims that the role of Autolycus is superfluous (1918, pp. 293–4). Such a charge is obtuse. Although Autolycus has little to do in the plot, his impact on stage is out of all proportion – as the play's first recorded spectator, Simon Forman, attested (*Casebook*, p. 23). But in a sense Quiller-Couch has a point. If, at the end of IV.iv, the expectation is set up that Autolycus will help discover Perdita, it is odd that it gets reversed. This is to contradict a long tradition in the role he is playing, that of the ingenious low-life figure who enables the comic ending. Northrop Frye has termed such a figure the 'tricky slave', and sketched its history from ancient Greece up to Jeeves in the work of P.G. Wodehouse. His examples from Shakespeare include Puck and Ariel (1957, pp. 173–4). Yet the tricky slave of *The Winter's Tale* is denied his expected triumph.

This anti-climax looks fully deliberate. When Autolycus next enters, in V.ii, he can only ask others what has happened and for once he has to keep silence for most of the scene. Left alone after over a hundred lines with nothing to say he ruefully explains how he missed his chance. Thanks to Perdita's and Florizel's seasickness while on board – an ironic, realistic, detail – 'this mystery remained undiscovered' [V.ii.118]. The point is rubbed in by the entrance of Shepherd and Clown to whom he has done an involuntary good turn. Here occurs a wonderful reversal usually spoiled in the theatre. Stage tradition has it that Autolycus continue true to form, picking pockets now newly enriched. John Russell Brown suggests with a little more subtlety that 'dejection for a clown is a new ploy, even if it appears unassumed' (1966, p. 102), but he also endorses the traditional comic business. Instead the dramatic point is to place Autolycus in the same relation to Shepherd and Clown as they were previously to him. No wonder he expects the worst: 'I humbly beseech you, sir, to pardon me all the faults I have committed to your worship, and to give me your good report

to the Prince my master' [145–7]. The beauty of the reversal
consists in the fact that he is forgiven, and forgiven because
Shepherd and Clown take their new-found gentility seriously:
'we must be gentle, now we are gentlemen' [148-9]. Russell Brown
argues that the scene gives Autolycus the final exit, and with it
every chance of the last laugh. But the text suggests otherwise,
the Clown beckoning to Autolycus to accompany them: 'Come,
follow us: we'll be thy good masters' [169].

One reason why Autolycus has so often beguiled readers
and performers is that the Shepherd and Clown are usually
taken to be bumpkins who are proper comic targets. Or worse
– Dover Wilson found 'a streak of meanness' in the Clown,
and ridiculously inferred that he suspected Perdita of trying to
squander his inheritance (1931, pp. 172, 163). True, the two have
their share of the comedy, and the title 'Clown', which refers to a
kind of acting role rather than to a yokel type, shows this is right.
But their lines do not justify the Mummerset accents (and much
else) which they so often get in performance. The Shepherd, who
is the only one of the country characters except Perdita to be
given blank verse, has dignity as well as the generosity which his
son shares. With his venerable 'fourscore three' years [IV.iv.450]
he honours such moral traditions as charity and hospitality; and
his son differs chiefly in his callow, impulsive youth. Shakespeare
does not sentimentalise either. But he does suggest that they are
not to be taken for granted, and that the values they stand for are
important. In these respects, as Charles Barber argued (1964), the
country has a message for the court.

15   Restoring women

In no other of Shakespeare's plays are there three central roles
for women of such variety and dramatic importance as those of
Hermione, Paullina and Perdita. The fact stands out not only
because before the Restoration all female parts on the professional
stage were taken by males. Also unusual is that *The Winter's Tale*
disdains any of the erotic games of cross-dressing played in several
of Shakespeare's earlier comedies, such as *The Merchant of Venice*
or *As You Like It*, where boy plays girl plays boy. All three of its
women's roles are unequivocally female.

Of these Hermione's role is now often and oddly sold short.

Gemma Jones helps explain why in her fine essay on the part, which she played with the Royal Shakespeare Company in 1981. She candidly admits that at first she was reluctant to accept it, because it seemed to offer little which might satisfy her 'egotistical desire . . . as an actress to impress; to act devious, clever, complicated and interesting' (1985, p. 157). Hermione's goodness seemed too limiting. The academic version of this view is represented by those who seek motives for Leontes's jealousy in some aspect of his wife's behaviour. Norman Nathan suggests that there is 'some slight unbalance in her nature', and that she 'apparently treated Polixenes with less reserve and with greater personal regard than she had displayed before other men' (1968, pp. 21, 24). Similarly, A. L. French argues that 'in her words to Polixenes she is very obviously using her sex', and that this may even have a 'nasty edge' (1972, pp. 139–40, 141). But this kind of interpretation is a dead end. Though it makes a kind of sense of the sequence between Hermione, Polixenes and Leontes, it makes nonsense of the rest of the play. If evidence is needed, there is the theatrical experiment Gemma Jones describes from rehearsal:

> We improvise my playing the first scene guilty – as if Leontes has justifiable cause for suspicion – which is fun to play (very wicked and delicious), but observation on the exercise is that it is perverse and destructive to attempt to give Leontes a rational jealousy. Hermione must personify all that is pure and right in order to illuminate the irrationality of his jealousy and the extent of his loss.   (1985, pp. 158–9)

Jones sums up her prescription for playing the statue scene in the words: '"the simpler the better" seems to be the answer' (p. 162). And there is a practical reason why the part was written this way. Given even the highly skilled actors Shakespeare could depend on for his female roles – as with Cleopatra – there were limits to the demands he could impose in a play requiring three of them. As Michael Jamieson has remarked, Shakespeare 'seems to have required of the boy-actress playing Hermione the simplest effects, which – on a stage dominated by the insanely jealous Leontes – would have been the more telling in dignity and calm' (1968, p. 82).

Nevertheless, practical pressures alone hardly account for the creation of Hermione. Other qualities of the role point up its special importance and interest. Although the text does not suggest that Hermione's behaviour directly provokes Leontes's jealousy, it does offer two possible ways of understanding it. First, there is the fact discussed in Section 11 that Hermione falls into suspicion for the very fullness and warmth with which she treats her guest. In effect she is imprisoned in a contradiction. Her duty as hostess is to make the king's friend welcome, and not to do so would be to show 'Both disobedience and ingratitude' [III.ii.67]. Yet the welcome makes the king mad. Hermione's last word before his explosive aside is 'friend' [I.ii.108]. This is entirely innocent, but, as Ernest Schanzer points out, it had the secondary meaning of 'lover' (1969, p. 24). With such social and linguistic doubleness she stands hardly a chance.

A second and even more dangerous contradiction is revealed by Hermione's dialogue with Polixenes after she has persuaded him to stay. Polixenes describes his childhood with Leontes as one of perfect innocence, and Hermione takes him up wittily: 'By this we gather / You have tripped since' [I.ii.75–6]. He responds, in effect, by agreeing: 'O my most sacred lady, / Temptations have since then been born to's' [76–7], pointing out that he and Leontes had not then met their wives. Hermione is quick to pick him up on what this implies: 'Of this make no conclusion, lest you say / Your queen and I are devils' [81–2]. In doing so she highlights a crucial contradiction in which women, to use his own words, are seen at one and the same time both as 'sacred' and as 'Temptations'. It is this fissure in male attitudes to women which immediately opens up in Leontes's jealousy. John Dover Wilson was the first to observe that the words which follow could have a dangerous double meaning if heard out of context by Leontes (1931, p. 133): 'Th' offences we have made you do we'll answer, / If you first sinned with us, and that with us / You did continue fault, and that you slipped not / With any but with us' [83–6]. Yet if Leontes does misinterpret these words it is a terrible irony, for Hermione is referring to the Christian view of marriage. Her words are a colloquial version of St Paul's authoritative statement: 'It is good for a man not to touch a woman. Nevertheless, to avoid fornication, let every man have his own wife, and let every woman have her own husband' (I Corinthians vii.1–2).

However lighthearted his speeches, Polixenes identifies women as the source of sexual temptation and sin. Later, and consistently, he will accuse Perdita of seducing his son. Leontes's jealousy shows him living the same belief to destruction. But if part of the play's achievement is to suggest how such an appalling wrong comes about, another part is to show how it is faced and finally overcome. It is important that the next scene in which Hermione appears [II.i] presents her in a domestic, family setting. This is not just for dramatic contrast when Leontes furiously breaks in, powerful though the effect is, but to emphasise her female care and nurturance. She is capable of empathy even in responding to his violent accusation: 'How will this grieve you, / When you shall come to clearer knowledge, that / You thus have published me!' [II.i.96–8]. Yet Shakespeare does not exploit the convention of female proneness to weeping. Hermione asserts her innocence with straightforward, uncompromising dignity.

This is also Hermione's keynote in the trial scene. Properly spoken in the theatre, her speeches in self-defence have a passionate, thrilling conviction. The verse Shakespeare gives her could hardly contrast more strongly with the tortured rhythms he gives Leontes. There is a magnificently controlled use of the line-unit: 'You speak a language that I understand not' [III.ii.79]; 'The bug which you would fright me with I seek' [91]; 'The innocent milk in its most innocent mouth' [99]. As also in the second of these examples there is a powerful use of simple antithesis: 'Tell me what blessing I have here alive / That I should fear to die' [106–7]. At a more complex level there is a firm, cogent balancing of word and verse: 'I doubt not then but innocence shall make / False accusation blush, and tyranny / Tremble at patience' [29–31]. Here the words 'innocence' and 'patience' enclose 'False accusation' and 'tyranny', forming a tight chiastic unit; while the first of two run-on lines suspends object from verb ('make / False accusation') and the second, with powerful alliteration, verb from subject ('tyranny / Tremble'). Though I cannot give an extended analysis, I emphasise in detail the force of Hermione's defence because critics tend to neglect it and it is not always done justice in production. It demands recognition not only for its magnificent use of language and theatre, but for its compelling affirmation of female dignity and integrity.

When Hermione faints at the news of her son's death, Paulina carries on that affirmation. Her role is especially striking in that it is wholly Shakespeare's invention. John Lucas compares her with other companion women in Shakespeare who are rarely to be found in his sources, such as Nerissa in *The*

Merchant of Venice, Beatrice in *Much Ado About Nothing*, and Emilia – who has a namesake in *The Winter's Tale* – in *Othello*. What all these women offer, he points out, 'is companionship to heroines who are isolated in and vulnerable to a male-dominated society' (1982, p. 11). He adds that Paulina goes further in that, denied her friend's presence, she insists passionately on speaking for her. She becomes what Simon Shepherd has termed a 'warrior woman' (1981, pp. 1–2).

If through Hermione Shakespeare exposes contradictions in male attitudes to women, through Paulina he demystifies the stereotype of the scold. In Section 13 I discussed how the stereotype is subverted when only Paulina has the courage to challenge Leontes directly. As the play continues, Shakespeare transforms it utterly. Paulina not only stands up for her friend, apparently dead, but becomes the voice of Leontes's conscience. In both instances she takes over roles which were – in many ways still are – typically thought of as male. First, her speech proclaiming Hermione's death is a triumph of militant defiance. She does not know that Leontes has repented, though dramatic licence allows her to include in her list of his crimes his wrong to Camillo. Yet she begins by asking him to do his worst against her, parodying his earlier threats: 'What wheels? Rack? Fires? What flaying? Boiling / In leads or oils?' [III.ii.174–5]. She goes on to insult him both with the familiar 'thou' and 'thy', and with a word ('fool') which several eighteenth-century editors could not accept as addressed to a king (Furness, 1964, p. 134). Second, once she has acknowledged his contrition, she follows Camillo in becoming his closest advisor and counsellor. When the play returns to Sicilia, it shows her acting as perpetual guard to his conscience and as reminder of Hermione. Though the courtiers protest [V.i.20–34, 73, 75], Leontes gives a different account: 'O grave and good Paulina, the great comfort/ That I have had of thee!' [V.iii.1–2].

This speech prepares for the third conventionally male role which Paulina takes over, and the most important. In offering Leontes the chance to reaffirm his faith in Hermione she becomes, even more than Camillo, producer of the play's resolution. The only precedent in Shakespeare for a woman exercising such a determining influence is Portia in *The Merchant of Venice*. But in defeating Shylock Portia has to abandon her femininity, while what Paulina contributes is a triumph of female creation.

Northrop Frye has pointed out that, although since the Greeks Western comedy has turned on the triumph of the younger generation, Shakespeare's last plays reverse the emphasis (1965, pp. 87–8). *The Winter's Tale* culminates not in the marriage of Perdita and Florizel, nor even in Perdita's restoration to Leontes, but in the reunion of Leontes and Hermione. Yet *The Winter's Tale* also stands out from the other last plays in that it is women who take the largest part in its resolution. It is a play not just about women restored (Perdita, Hermione), but about restoring women – both in the sense that Paulina, Perdita and Hermione enable restoration, and in the sense that it gives back to women an essential role and identity from which men dispossess them.

Here the pastoral scene in IV.iv has a vital function, and especially through two thematic and structural parallels. Early in the play Polixenes describes to Hermione the golden world of childhood innocence he enjoyed with Leontes, when it seemed there could be no change, 'But such a day tomorrow as today, / And to be boy eternal' [64–5]. As pastoral traditionally shows a version of paradise on earth, the pastoral scene presents a social equivalent for this idyllic memory. But the parallel is doubly significant. First, the shepherds' life is only lightly idealised, open as it is to raids not just from bear and trickster but from an angry king. As Antigonus discovers, and as Polixenes threatens, death also lives in Arcadia. Similarly S. L. Bethell observes that, while in conventional pastoral flowers bloom all the year round, here they have their seasons (1956, p. 209; see Perdita's wonderful speech at IV.iv. 112–29). Second, the country's transforming influence is needed for the court's regeneration. In this consists the importance of Perdita's role.

Again there is a crucial parallel with the play's beginning. Perdita renews her mother's role as hostess, but in doing so draws out the best in Florizel as well as the worst in Polixenes. What is striking about her words and behaviour is their innocent eroticism. The verse Shakespeare gives her has an impulsive, buoyant energy, and her language has a downright directness as when she briskly dismisses Polixenes's smart horticultural philosophy:

> I'll not put
> The dibble in earth to set one slip of them:
> No more than, were I painted, I would wish

This youth to say 'twere well, and only therefore
Desire to breed by me.

[IV.iv. 99–103]

Perdita not only rejects artifice, but shows a wholly and rightly un-embarrassed recognition of the sexual in her relation to Florizel. When he asks humorously, 'What, like a corse?' in response to her promise to cover him with flowers, she replies: 'No, like a bank for Love to lie and play on, / Not like a corse; or if, not to be buried, / But quick and in mine arms' [129–32]. This frank, warm avowal of sexual feeling is followed by the glorious poetry in which Florizel celebrates her natural grace and spontaneity [135–46]. But as always in this play the effect of the verse is not only local. The presentation of Perdita reasserts with overwhelming conviction what was denied in her mother.

This parallel raises the question how much Perdita's qualities owe to royal birth and how much to country upbringing. One way of focusing it is to ask whether in the theatre she should be played with an accent. Conventionally, Perdita is made to speak standard or upper-class English, and the Shepherd and Clown some absurd theatrical dialect. There is little basis in the text for such a distinction, especially as the Shepherd mainly speaks a dignified blank verse. Neither is there any basis in the action. It is a tradition of rural hospitality which Perdita carries on, as described in the Shepherd's speech about his wife [55–62], and her sense of honour is as strict as his. Either all of the country characters should have accents, including Perdita, or none. Equally Perdita is right to speak up for herself and her adopted family against their social superiors. As she says of Polixenes, 'The selfsame sun that shines upon his court / Hides not his visage from our cottage, but / Looks on alike' [441–3]. That this is not a sentimental commonplace is borne out by the dramatic action, which proves the Shepherd a better man than either king.

The arc followed by the play may be traced through the varying meanings of the word 'affection'. It first comes up in the opening scene, when Camillo pays tribute to the 'affection' which rooted between Leontes and Polixenes [I.i.23]. Next, in one of his first paroxysms of jealousy, Leontes has the striking line: 'Affection, thy intention stabs the centre' [I.ii.138]. In Leontes's fantasy the sense of 'kind feeling' or 'loving attachment' (OED, sense 6) gives way to that of 'feeling as opposed to reason; passion, lust' (OED, sense 3). It is in IV.iv, and thanks to Perdita, that the earlier benign meaning is restored. Camillo says that Florizel's declaration of love for Perdita 'shows a sound affection' [IV.iv.376]. But what Florizel says himself is more arresting: 'From my succession wipe me, father, I / Am heir to my affection'; especially when, to Camillo's 'Be advised', he replies:

> I am, and by my fancy. If my reason
> Will thereto be obedient, I have reason;
> If not, my senses, better pleased with madness,
> Do bid it welcome.

(477-82)

Once more the play presents a parallel between its second and first parts, or rather a reversal. While Leontes was unhinged by madness of 'affection', Florizel affirms its natural goodness and rightness. The link is confirmed when the latter chooses the same word in appealing to the former for help: 'With thought of such affections / Step forth mine advocate' [V.i.219–20]; and near the end the Third Gentleman speaks of the 'greediness of affection' with which Leontes and the others go to see Hermione's statue [V.ii.100]. The importance of this verbal progress consists in its vital relevance to the final scene. It is there that Paulina suggests to Leontes that his 'fancy' may cause the statue to move, and he welcomes the possibility: 'No settled senses of the world can match / The pleasure of that madness' [V.iii.60, 72–3]. Fancy, madness – Leontes can now endorse with Florizel the power of loving attachment. It had been his own failure to honour that power in others which led to its insane, murderous perversion in himself. Men, especially men in high rank, are normally associated with a different kind of power. Leontes and Polixenes enjoyed their mutual affection in childhood, until it had to give way to 'their more mature dignities and royal necessities' [I.i.24–5]. It is most of all through women, and indifference to rank, that the proper power of affection is restored.

16   The final scene

That restoration is designed to affect not only the stage spectators but the audience. In this the statue scene has its crucial importance, and it is given every chance, through verse and action, to succeed. First, irrational though it seems, the sequence has many naturalising touches. It is possible to recognise these by considering the different responses available to a spectator who knows the play and to one who does not. All commentators agree that in *The Winter's Tale* Shakespeare suspends his usual practice of taking the audience into his confidence when he strongly suggests that Hermione is actually dead. The combined effect of Paulina's speeches in III.ii and Antigonus's vision in III.iii seems conclusive; and members of earlier audiences who knew *Pandosto* had no reason to expect the queen to survive. It follows that for first-time spectators Hermione's recovery should be wholly unexpected. However, Paulina has some ambiguous words in V.i. that imply the possibility of Hermione's restoration [40, 47, 69–70, 73–5, 76–81, 82–4], and that possibility slowly dawns in V.iii. What this suggests is that for members of audiences who know the play the dramatic impact does not depend on surprise. Part of the reason for this is also within the experience available to first-time spectators, in that the response of the onstage audience is hardly less powerful and moving than the sight of Hermione coming to life. Further, as Fitzroy Pyle points out, in V.iii Shakespeare keeps a careful balance between miraculous effect and justifying detail (1969, pp. 126–32; see Section 6 above). For those who know the play Paulina's ambiguities fulfil a similar part in rendering the action plausible.

But such a word is too weak for a dramatic impact which can achieve great intensity in performance. The action gets its potential from two main sources which, at the same time, lend it conviction. First there is the unnerving aptness of the statue metaphor to what Hermione and Leontes have undergone. He has tried to condemn her, she has been dead to him. He has denied her very being, above all her femininity; she has become as stone. Metaphorically and humanly it is supremely apt that the woman he has treated as no person at all should return to him from the state of a mere, however lifelike, object. There is a double meaning when he expresses his shame at the impression of her warm life: 'Does not the stone rebuke me / For being more stone than it?' [V.iii.37–8].

Second, the language and action of the scene also convey total human conviction. It is natural that when Paulina first unveils the statue Leontes responds with stunned silence. What is extraordinary is the comic truth of his quick recognition that

'Hermione was not so much wrinkled, nothing / So agèd as this seems' [28–9]. Similarly, Paulina's words 'Do not shun her' [105] suggest that, naturally enough, he draws back in consternation when the statue starts to move. But his response on first touching Hermione, 'O, she's warm!' [109], risks bathos for a simple but overwhelming physical and emotional truth. His own comment pays tribute to its rightness: 'If this be magic, let it be an art / Lawful as eating' [110–11]. The responses of the others onstage are in every way consistent. Polixenes shows a generous care for Leontes by offering: 'Let him that was the cause of this have power/ To take off so much grief from you as he / Will piece up in himself' [54–6]. Leontes later reciprocates when Hermione understandably holds off from his friend: 'What! Look upon my brother. Both your pardons / That e'er I put between your holy looks / My ill suspicion' [147–9]. Paulina moves from self-possessed orchestrator of the scene to humorous commentator: 'That she is living, / Were it but told you, should be hooted at / Like an old tale: but it appears she lives, / Though yet she speak not' [115–18]. Then, just as humanly, her amused satisfaction at the happiness of the others gives way to self-pity at her own isolation: 'I, an old turtle, / Will wing me to some withered bough, and there / My mate, that's never to be found again, / Lament till I am lost' [132–5]. The immediate response from Leontes is humorous in more ways than one. Not only does his proposal to match her with Camillo meet her complaint aptly. It is also comic in allowing him for once an effective response.

Granville-Barker points out Shakespeare's tact in leaving much of what might have been said in the scene unspoken (1974, p. 22). Perdita is given little to say; Hermione a single speech, to her daughter. It is not simply the text which determines dramatic importance, especially in a scene which for the first time sets the play's three principal women together onstage. Visually and theatrically Hermione is the pivotal figure, and Paulina's importance as stage-manager is obvious. But it is only Perdita whom Hermione addresses, claiming the vital relation denied her. During the course of the action the three have undergone not only the primary roles available specifically to women: as daughter, betrothed, wife, mother, widow. They have also suffered roles inflicted on women by male ideology and power: suspected adultress, virago, witch, seductress. It is by reasserting their primary roles that they redeem not only themselves but the male world.

Like the play as a whole, the final scene has room for other readings than I have given here. It is one of the marks of great writing to open up a variety of possible meanings, allowing people in successive generations and even in different cultures to find in it a response to their own experience. This does not necessarily mean imposing perceptions which, in historical terms, simply falsify. Even history is hardly a given, but is itself actively produced by discovery and interpretation. Any critical act enters a dialogue, historically conditioned on both sides. Changing historical conditions bring different sides of a great artistic work to light.

This is above all true of a work of such powerful theatricality as *The Winter's Tale*. A play of surprise and paradox, it both presses questions on its audiences and challenges them to take the measure of what they see. The play is extraordinary not only in its combination of tragic and comic action but in its ability to hold both perspectives simultaneously. In this respect the mingled solemnity and humour of the final scene is wholly characteristic. When Leontes calls on Paulina and Camillo to marry, Shakespeare renews an ancient comic convention. Much of the humour lies in recognising its conventionality. The effect is in part to build an emotional bridge for the audience back to the real world outside the play. Not for the first time, there is a double-take in which the convention is offered as acceptable through recognition of conventionality. The result of Leontes's gesture cannot be to reassert the patriarchal dominance which the play has questioned. Rather the tone in which it is made is a tribute to the success with which patriarchy has been tamed.

References and Further Reading

THE list below is divided into eleven sections. Ten of these correspond to the sections of Part One, for convenience in finding details of each critical work discussed in them. The last is a general list of all other works mentioned, including those referred to in the Introduction and in Part Two. Most sections also offer suggestions for further reading, though the aim is to represent a range of material rather than a full bibliography. A few works necessarily appear more than once, though no references are repeated in the general section.

Dates given are those of the editions used. Where applicable dates of first editions are also indicated. Texts represented in Kenneth Muir's *Casebook* on the play are marked with an asterisk (*).

1 Contexts

Baldick, Chris, *The Social Mission of English Criticism, 1848–1932* (Oxford, 1983).

Bartholomeusz, Dennis, *The Winter's Tale in performance in England and America, 1611–1976* (Cambridge, 1982).

Eagleton, Terry, *Literary Theory: an Introduction* (Oxford, 1983).

Knight, G. Wilson, *Shakespearian Production: with especial reference to the Tragedies* (London, 1st edn 1964;1968).

* Muir, Kenneth (ed.), *Shakespeare: The Winter's Tale*, Casebook Series (London, 1968).

Pafford, J.H.P. (ed.), *The Winter's Tale*, New Arden edn (London, 1963).

2   Evaluation

Baldick, Chris, *The Social Mission of English Criticism, 1848–1932* (Oxford, 1983).

* Bethell, S.L., *The Winter's Tale: A Study* (London, 1947).
* Coghill, Nevill, 'Six Points of Stage-Craft in *The Winter's Tale*', *Shakespeare Survey*, 11 (1958) 31–41.

Furness, Horace Howard (ed.), *The Winter's Tale*, New Variorum edn (New York, 1st edn 1898; 1964).

* MacNeice, Louis, 'Autolycus', in Muir (1968) pp. 232–3.

Quiller-Couch, Sir Arthur, 'The Winter's Tale', *Shakespeare's Workmanship* (London, 1918) pp. 282–99.

Further Reading

Bonjour, Adrien, 'The Final Scene of *The Winter's Tale*', *English Studies*, 33 (1952) 193–208.

Matchett, William H., 'Some Dramatic Techniques in "The Winter's Tale"', *Shakespeare Survey*, 22 (1969) 93–107.

Muir, Kenneth, 'The Conclusion of *The Winter's Tale*', *The Singularity of Shakespeare and Other Essays* (Liverpool, 1977) pp. 76–91.

* Tillyard, E.M.W., *Shakespeare's Last Plays* (London, 1st edn 1938; 1968).

3   Imagery, symbolism, myth

* Bethell, S.L., *The Winter's Tale: A Study* (London, 1947).

Bethell, S.L. (ed.), *The Winter's Tale*, New Clarendon Shakespeare edn (Oxford, 1956).

Clemen, Wolfgang, *The Development of Shakespeare's Imagery* (2nd edn, London, 1977: 1st edn published in German, 1936).

* Knight, G. Wilson, '"Great Creating Nature": An Essay on *The Winter's Tale*', *The Crown of Life: Essays in Interpretation of Shakespeare's Final Plays* (London, 1st edn 1947; 1965) pp. 76–128.

Spurgeon, Caroline F.E., *Shakespeare's Imagery and What It Tells Us* (Cambridge, 1st edn 1935; 1958).

* Traversi, Derek, *'The Winter's Tale', Shakespeare: The Last Phase* (London, 1st edn 1954; 1965) pp. 105–92.

Further Reading

Mulhern, Francis, *The Moment of 'Scrutiny'* (London, 1979).
Tinkler, F.C., '"The Winter's Tale"', *Scrutiny*, 5 (1937) 344–64.
Traversi, Derek, 'The Winter's Tale', *An Approach to Shakespeare*, vol.2 (London, 1st edn 1938; 1969) pp. 282–302.

4   Allegory and theme

Bryant, J.A., Jr, 'Shakespeare's Allegory: *The Winter's Tale*', *Sewanee Review*, 63 (1955) 202–22.
Edwards, Philip, 'Shakespeare's Romances, 1900–1957', *Shakespeare Survey*, 11 (1958) 1–18.
* Ewbank, Inga-Stina, 'The Triumph of Time in "The Winter's Tale"', *Review of English Literature*, 5 (1964) 83–100.
Fowler, Alastair, 'Leontes' Contrition and the Repair of Nature', *Essays and Studies*, 31 (1978) 36–64.
Levin, Richard, *New Readings vs. Old Plays: Recent Trends in the Reinterpretation of English Renaissance Drama* (Chicago, 1979).
Levin, Richard, 'The Relation of External Evidence to the Allegorical and Thematic Interpretation of Shakespeare', *Shakespeare Studies*, 13 (1980) 1–29.
Tayler, E.W., *Nature and Art in Renaissance Literature* (New York and London, 1964).
Wickham, Glynne, 'Romance and Emblem: A Study in the Dramatic Structure of *The Winter's Tale*', in David Galloway (ed.), *The Elizabethan Theatre*, III (Toronto and London, 1973) pp. 82–99.

Further Reading

Egan, Robert, *Drama Within Drama: Shakespeare's Sense of His Art in King Lear, The Winter's Tale and the Tempest* (New York and London, 1975).

Yates, Frances A., *Shakespeare's Last Plays: A New Approach* (London, 1975).

5   Genre and convention

Colie, Rosalie L., *Shakespeare's Living Art* (Princeton, 1974) pp. 261–83.
Frye, Northrop, *Anatomy of Criticism* (Princeton, 1957).
* Frye, Northrop, 'Recognition in *The Winter's Tale*', *Fables of Identity: Studies in Poetic Mythology* (New York, 1963) pp. 107–18.
Frye, Northrop, *A Natural Perspective: The Development of Shakespearean Comedy and Romance* (New York and London, 1965).
Hartwig, Joan, *Shakespeare's Comic Vision* (Baton Rouge, 1972).
Uphaus, Robert W., 'The Issues of *The Winter's Tale*', *Beyond Tragedy: Structure and Experience in Shakespeare's Romances* (Lexington, 1981).
Wells, Stanley, 'Shakespeare and Romance', *Later Shakespeare*, John Russell Brown and Bernard Harris (eds), Stratford-upon-Avon Studies, 8 (London, 1966) pp. 48–79.

Further Reading

Blissett, William, 'This Wide Gap of Time: *The Winter's Tale*', *English Literary Renaissance*, 1 (1971) 52–70.
Frey, Charles, *Shakespeare's Vast Romance: A study of The Winter's Tale* (Columbia and London, 1980).
Gesner, Carol, *Shakespeare and the Greek Romance* (Lexington, 1970).
Leavis, F.R.,'The Criticism of Shakespeare's Late Plays: A Caveat', in *The Common Pursuit* (1st publ. 1942; London, 1952) pp. 173–81.
Martz, Louis L., 'Shakespeare's humanist enterprise: *The Winter's Tale*', *English Renaissance Studies Presented to Dame Helen Gardner*, ed. John Carey (Oxford, 1980) pp. 114–31.
Riemer, A.P., *Antic Fables: Patterns of Evasion in Shakespeare's Comedies* (Manchester, 1980).
Wolff, Samuel Lee, *The Greek Romances in Elizabethan Prose Fiction* (New York, 1912).

6   Structure and source

Hirsh, James E., *The Structure of Shakespearean Scenes* (New Haven and London, 1981).
Pyle, Fitzroy, *The Winter's Tale: A Commentary on the Structure* (London, 1969).
* Schanzer, Ernest, 'The Structural Pattern of "The Winter's Tale"', *Review of English Literature*, 5 (1964) 72–82.
Schanzer, Ernest (ed.), *The Winter's Tale*, New Penguin Shakespeare edn (Harmondsworth, 1969).

Further Reading

Bullough, Geoffrey (ed.), *Narrative and Dramatic Sources of Shakespeare*, vol. VIII (London, 1975) pp. 115–233.
Honigmann, E.A.J., 'Secondary Sources of *The Winter's Tale*', *Philological Quarterly*, 34 (1955) 27–38.

7   Marxism

Barber, Charles, '*The Winter's Tale* and Jacobean Society', in Arnold Kettle (ed.), *Shakespeare in a Changing World* (London, 1964).

Further Reading

Craig, David (ed.), *Marxists on Literature: An Anthology* (Harmondsworth, 1975).
Eagleton, Terry, *Marxism and Literary Criticism* (London, 1976).
Kettle, Arnold (ed.), *Shakespeare in a Changing World* (London, 1964).

8   Psychoanalysis

Barber, C.L., '"Thou that beget'st him that did thee beget": Transformation in "Pericles" and "The Winter's Tale"', *Shakespeare Survey*, 22 (1969) 59–67.

Reid, Stephen, 'The Winter's Tale', American Imago, 27 (1970) 263–78.

Schwartz, Murray M., 'Leontes' Jealousy in The Winter's Tale', in Leonard Tennenhouse (ed.), The Practice of Psychoanalytic Criticism (Detroit, 1976) pp. 202–25.

Stewart, J.I.M., Character and Motive in Shakespeare (1st edn 1949; London, 1965) pp. 30–7.

Further Reading

Nuttall, A.D., William Shakespeare: The Winter's Tale (London, 1966) pp. 14–29.

Schwartz, Murray M., 'The Winter's Tale: Loss and Tranformation', American Imago, 32 (1975) 145–99.

Wright, Elizabeth, Psychoanalytic Criticism: Theory in Practice (London, 1984).

9   Feminism

Asp, Carolyn, 'Shakespeare's Paulina and the Consolatio Tradition', Shakespeare Studies, 11 (1978) 145–58.

French, Marilyn, Shakespeare's Division of Experience (1st edn 1981; London, 1983).

Gourlay, Patricia Southard, "'O my most sacred lady": Female Metaphor in The Winter's Tale', English Literary Renaissance, 5 (1975) 375–95.

Jardine, Lisa, Still Harping on Daughters: Women and Drama in the Age of Shakespeare (Brighton, 1983).

Further Reading

Cook, Judith, Women in Shakespeare (London, 1980).

Dusinberre, Juliet, Shakespeare and the Nature of Women (London and Basingstoke, 1975).

Shepherd, Simon, Amazons and Warrior Women: Varieties of Feminism in Seventeenth-Century Drama (Brighton, 1981).

10 Performance

Bartholomeusz, Dennis, *The Winter's Tale in performance in England and America, 1611–1976* (Cambridge, 1982).
Draper, R.P., *The Winter's Tale: Text and Performance* (London and Basingstoke, 1985).
Lamb, Charles, 'On the Tragedies of Shakespeare, Considered with Reference to Their Fitness for Stage Representation', in D. Nichol Smith (ed.), *Shakespeare Criticism: A Selection* (1st publ. 1811; London, 1916) pp. 215–40.
Muir, Kenneth, '*The Winter's Tale*', in *Shakespeare's Comic Sequence* (Liverpool, 1979) pp. 163–75.

Further Reading

Male, David A., *Shakespeare on Stage: The Winter's Tale* (Cambridge, 1984).

11 General

Adams, Douglas, *The Hitch Hiker's Guide to the Galaxy* (London, 1979).
Bateson, F.W., 'How Old was Leontes?', *Essays and Studies*, 31 (1978) 65–74.
Biggins, Dennis, '"Exit pursued by a Beare": A Problem in *The Winter's Tale*', *Shakespeare Quarterly*, 13 (1962) 3–13.
Bohannan, Laura, 'Miching Mallecho: that means witchcraft', John Morris (ed.), *From the Third Programme: A Ten-Years' Anthology* (London, 1956) pp. 174–89.
Bradley, A.C., *Shakespearean Tragedy* (London, 1904).
Brown, John Russell, 'Playing for Laughs: The Last Plays', in *Shakespeare's Plays in Performance* (London, 1966) pp. 91–112.
Brown, John Russell, *Free Shakespeare* (1st edn 1974; London, 1978).
Eastman, Arthur M., *A Short History of Shakespearean Criticism* (New York, 1968).
French, A.L., 'Leontes' Jealousy', in *Shakespeare and the Critics* (Cambridge, 1972) pp. 135–43.
Granville-Barker, Harley, '*The Winter's Tale*', in Edward M. Moore (ed.), *Prefaces to Shakespeare*, vol.VI (1st edn 1912; London, 1974) pp. 19–25.

James, D.G., 'The Failure of the Ballad-Makers', in *Scepticism and Poetry* (London, 1937) pp. 205–41.

Jamieson, Michael, 'Shakespeare's Celibate Stage: The Problem of Accommodation to the Boy-Actors in *As You Like It, Antony and Cleopatra*, and *The Winter's Tale*', in Gerald Eades Bentley (ed.), *The Seventeenth-Century Stage* (Chicago and London, 1968) pp. 70–93.

Jones, Gemma, 'Hermione in *The Winter's Tale*', in *Players of Shakespeare*, ed. Philip Brockbank (Cambridge, 1985) pp. 153–65.

Lucas, John, 'Freedom and Hospitality in *The Winter's Tale*', *Sixth Form Shakespeare Conference Papers*, Department of English and Drama, Loughborough University (1982) pp. 1–21.

Nathan, Norman, 'Leontes' Provocation', *Shakespeare Quarterly*, 19 (1968) 19–24.

Quiller-Couch, Sir Arthur and Wilson, J. Dover (eds), *The Winter's Tale*, New Cambridge Shakespeare edn (Cambridge, 1931).

Smith, Jonathan, 'The Language of Leontes', *Shakespeare Quarterly*, 19 (1968) 317–27.

Stoppard, Tom, *Rosencrantz and Guildenstern are Dead* (London, 1967).

Index

55